ROUTLEDGE LIBRARY EDITIONS: GERMAN HISTORY

Volume 19

THE EVOLUTION OF GERMANY

THE EVOLUTION OF GERMANY

JOHN A. HAWGOOD

NEW YORK AND LONDON

First published in 1955 by Methuen & Co. Ltd.

This edition first published in 2020
by Routledge
52 Vanderbilt Avenue, New York, NY 10017

and by Routledge
2 Park Square, Milton Park, Abingdon, Oxon OX14 4RN

Routledge is an imprint of the Taylor & Francis Group, an informa business

© 1955 John A. Hawgood

All rights reserved. No part of this book may be reprinted or reproduced or utilised in any form or by any electronic, mechanical, or other means, now known or hereafter invented, including photocopying and recording, or in any information storage or retrieval system, without permission in writing from the publishers.

Trademark notice: Product or corporate names may be trademarks or registered trademarks, and are used only for identification and explanation without intent to infringe.

British Library Cataloguing in Publication Data
A catalogue record for this book is available from the British Library

ISBN: 978-0-367-02813-8 (Set)
ISBN: 978-0-429-27806-8 (Set) (ebk)
ISBN: 978-0-367-24376-0 (Volume 19) (hbk)
ISBN: 978-0-367-24380-7 (Volume 19) (pbk)
ISBN: 978-0-429-28213-3 (Volume 19) (ebk)

Publisher's Note
The publisher has gone to great lengths to ensure the quality of this reprint but points out that some imperfections in the original copies may be apparent.

Disclaimer
The publisher has made every effort to trace copyright holders and would welcome correspondence from those they have been unable to trace.

The Evolution
of Germany

by
John A. Hawgood

METHUEN & CO LTD, LONDON
36 Essex Street, Strand, WC2

First published in 1955

1.1

CATALOGUE NO. 4468/U

*Printed and bound in Great Britain by
Jarrold and Sons Ltd, Norwich*

PREFACE

TO men and women of today German history is an enigma which was not presented to earlier ages. Looking back from the middle of the twentieth century upon the last hundred years, we see Germany as the great disturber of the peace of Europe and of the world, but for the generations that lived from 1715 to 1815 the great disturber was France, while, from about 1620 to 1720, the now innocuous and peace-loving Sweden was the scourge of most of Europe. Before that the great bogy was Spain, and throughout the fifteenth century and well into the sixteenth it was the Ottoman Turks.

During these earlier centuries—after the break-up of the power of the medieval German emperors in the mid-thirteenth century—nobody in Europe really feared Germany or the German people. Right up to the end of the eighteenth century and into the early years of the nineteenth, their power for good and evil was treated with scorn. 'The Germans are the Old Men of Europe,' wrote Madame de Stael. No doubt, if a man had written *De L'Allemagne*, he would have characterized them as 'the Old Women of Europe'!

In fact, until less than a hundred years ago, 'The German Problem', in so far as it existed at all, existed only for Germans. Bismarck turned it into a European problem, and his successors—William II by blundering and maladroitness, and Adolf Hitler deliberately and fanatically—into a problem for all the world.

When we seek to survey the whole course of German history, ever since the concept 'Germany' first came into existence, we have always to remember that the German problem has undergone this historically recent metamorphosis, and that its urgency and its seriousness are relatively new phenomena.

Even Victorian England did not *fear* (though she may have disapproved of and distrusted) Bismarck's Germany in the way that Edwardian England genuinely came to fear the Germany of William II. Nor did the Russia of Nicholas I fear Germany and her ambitions in the way that the Russia of Nicholas II (and Stalin) came to do so. The Frenchman's fear of Germany is of short duration, compared with the German's very well-founded fear of France for centuries before 1870. Certain German states were formidable enough from time to time—and Prussia started to be a force to be reckoned with during the seventeenth century under the Great Elector—but even Prussia was not reckoned a great power until she had unified Germany under her leadership in the nineteenth century. Frederick the Great performed wonders of aggression and chicanery with relatively meagre resources compared with those of the Habsburg Monarchy of Maria Theresa (only to a very partial extent, either then or later, a 'German' state), of the France of Louis XV, of the Britain of George II or of the Russia of Catherine the Great. For a time Prussia, under the hammer-blows of Napoleonic generalship and statecraft, came in the early years of the nineteenth century very close to that extinction which the once-great Polish state had suffered a few years earlier, and no historian, writing in the year 1806, of that state which had become 'rotten before it was ripe' would have dared to prophesy that, only sixty years later, Prussia would be one of the five great powers of Europe, or that 135 years later Germany would be dominating Europe even more completely than did Napoleonic France after Austerlitz.

PREFACE

We have in recent years had a surfeit of writings in English on 'The Problem' of Germany. There has been a tendency to look at Germany's whole development as if it only mattered for explaining this 'Problem'. Such a position is understandable, but it is a somewhat narrow one.

While 'The Problem' of nineteenth- and twentieth-century Germany will not be lost sight of in the survey that follows, an attempt will be made to remember that this problem has not always existed, and that Germany had some fifteen hundred years of previous history with an entirely different (if even more complicated) pattern to it.

It does not seem to the present writer essential to analyse happenings in, say, tenth-century Germany, only for their relevance for explaining the situation of twentieth-century Germany, though it may be that some of them *are* relevant for this purpose. On the other hand, he is only too conscious that a majority of his readers are likely to be far more interested in the Third Reich than in the Holy Roman Empire; in Bismarck than in Barbarossa; in the Zollverein than in the Golden Bull; and up to a point he has felt it possible to indulge this interest. But it would have resulted only in distortion if he had ignored or passed too lightly over the long and tortuous evolution of Germany up to the end of the Middle Ages in order to get more quickly to Luther and the Reformation, to Frederick the Great and the Liberation, to Bismarck and Unification. Important as these movements were in Germany's history, they have their roots in a more distant past. To concentrate too exclusively upon them—as was the temptation of an historian whose main interests previously lay in the modern period—would only have been to leave the story half-told—and less than half explained.

The historian today is often asked to perform the perhaps impossible task of writing at one and the same time a medieval chronicle and a modern leading article. A leading article sums up the situation today in the light of what may happen tomorrow, or a week or a year hence; the medieval chronicler treated the past and the present as being of equal relevance and importance—and ignored the future altogether.

The Evolution of Germany is not a chronicle; it is deliberately not even a purely chronological treatment; and it is the author's hope that it does not read like a leading article either. Above all it does not seek to be a comprehensive or even an outline history of Germany. A number of excellent books already exist to fill that need. The aim of this book is rather to serve as a guide to the better understanding of German history and of the German people, both for those who have studied them already and for those who are embarking upon such a study for the first time.

Birmingham,
    January 1954   J. A. H.

ACKNOWLEDGEMENTS

THIS small book is less the result of the three-year period of intermittent writing and reading that was needed for the production of the manuscript than of some thirty years' first-hand experience of Germany and the German people—the author's first schoolboy memories of Germany are of the inflation and the Ruhr occupation of the summer of 1923—and of the distillation of the learning and scholarship of those who have actually taught him about the problems of German history, as well as of those others who, through their publications, have given him almost equally valuable guidance and inspiration. Among the first group he would like particularly to mention his former teachers, the late Professor A. F. Pollard, the late Professor R. W. Seton-Watson and Professor Paul Vaucher in London, Professor Alfred Weber in Heidelberg, the late Professors A. F. Přibram, Josef Redlich and H. von Srbik in Vienna and (with special reference to the German-Americans) the late Dr. Joseph Schafe in Madison, Wisconsin.

Both through their works and through their personal help and advice, Dr. G. P. Gooch (the Nestor of British experts on German history), the late Sir Charles Grant Robertson and the late Professor Veit Valentin, contributed greatly to his understanding of German history, though they were never actually numbered among his academic teachers. Among those whose books he found specially useful (these books are listed among others on pages 195–202) were Professors G. Barraclough, Sir Lewis Namier, J. Haller, and the late Professor F. Lot,

Professors R. E. Dickinson, K. Reinhardt, Louis L. Snyder, and Dr. S. H. Steinberg, Professor E. Vermeil and Mr. John Wheeler-Bennett. During his period of government service (1939–45) he was privileged to meet and work with a less academic, and—to him—new and most refreshing type of expert on Germany, and he derived great benefit from contact with such men, coming from the world of affairs, as the late Charles Tower, F. Sefton Delmer and J. Emlyn Williams (journalism), D. Dem Dimancescu and the late President Beneš (diplomacy), Leonard Ingrams (banking) and Brigadiers Denis Daly and A. O. Scaife (regular army).

A Foreign Office former colleague, Professor Richard Samuel (now of Melbourne University), was kind enough to read and criticize part of the book in manuscript, as were also the author's present colleagues at Birmingham, Professor H. A. Cronne and Mr. D. R. Dudley, while Mrs. Anne Hutton wrestled successfully with his not always very decipherable handwriting in producing the typescript, and Alan Hawgood read through all the proofs. None of these is, of course, in any way responsible for the opinions expressed in the book or for its errors and defects, for which the author alone takes full responsibility.

Finally, he would like to acknowledge his gratitude to the General Editor of the Home Study Books, Dr. B. Ifor Evans, and to Mr. Peter Wait of Messrs. Methuens, for their encouragement and forbearance at all stages. Without their efforts the book would never have been finished, or indeed started. He can only hope that they will not live to regret them.

CONTENTS

CHAPTER		PAGE
	PREFACE	v
	ACKNOWLEDGEMENTS	ix

PART I. THE PEOPLES OF GERMANY

I	PREHISTORIC GERMANY	1
II	THE GERMANIC TRIBES	5
III	THE TRIBAL REGIONS	11
IV	NORTHERNERS AND SOUTHERNERS	15
V	EASTERNERS AND WESTERNERS	20
VI	GERMANS *versus* SLAVS	25
VII	GERMANS *versus* LATINS	31
VIII	GERMAN EXPANSION IN EUROPE	34

PART II. THE RESOURCES OF GERMANY

I	FOREST AND CLEARING	43
II	RIVER AND FORTRESS	47
III	THE PEASANTS AND THE LAND	54
IV	THE NOBILITY AND THEIR PRIVILEGES	63
V	THE TOWNSMEN AND THEIR LEAGUES	69
VI	INDUSTRIAL REVOLUTION	75
VII	POPULATION PROBLEMS	81

PART III. THE STATES OF GERMANY

| I | EAST AND WEST GERMANY SINCE 1945 | 89 |
| II | THE NAZI STATE: HITLER'S 'GREATER GERMANY' | 93 |

CHAPTER		PAGE
III	THE WEIMAR REPUBLIC	97
IV	THE HOHENZOLLERN EMPIRE: BISMARCK'S 'LESSER GERMANY'	102
V	THE PLAN FOR GERMAN UNITY OF 1848–49	106
VI	THE GERMAN *Bund* OF 1815–66	109
VII	NAPOLEON'S 'THIRD GERMANY': THE CONFEDERATION OF THE RHINE	112
VIII	THE CONSOLIDATION AND PARTITION OF PRUSSIA	115
IX	THE HABSBURG EMPIRE AS A 'GERMAN' POWER	120
X	THE LESSER STATES OF GERMANY	123

PART IV. GERMANY AND THE WORLD

I	GERMANY AND THE ROMAN EMPIRE	127
II	THE CAROLINGIAN EXPERIMENT	133
III	THE HOLY ROMAN EMPIRE: MYTH AND REALITY	139
IV	GERMANY AND THE MEDIEVAL PAPACY	143
V	GERMANY AND THE REFORMATION	149
VI	GERMANY AND THE RENAISSANCE	155
VII	GERMANY AND THE *Aufklärung*	159
VIII	GERMANY AND THE FRENCH REVOLUTION	166
IX	GERMANY AND THE EXPANSION OF EUROPE	171
X	GERMAN EMIGRATION: EUROPEAN AND OVERSEAS	179
XI	CONCLUSION: GERMANY'S PLACE IN AN INTEGRATED EUROPE	190
	READING LIST	195
	INDEX	203

MAPS

		PAGE
1	GERMANY, 1919–39 (*with 600-foot contour*)	*facing* 1
2	TRIBAL DUCHIES AND MARCHES OF THE GERMAN LANDS, A.D. 950–1250 (*with forest-free land shaded*)	8
3	THE DISTRIBUTION OF GERMAN DIALECTS	16
4	GERMAN MEDIEVAL BISHOPRICS (ABOUT A.D. 1000)	21
5	GERMANY'S EASTERN MARCHES	26
6	THE POLISH CORRIDOR, 1919–39	37
7	THE HANSEATIC LEAGUE AND THE TEUTONIC ORDER	39
8	POPULATION DENSITY IN CENTRAL EUROPE, 1938 (*map and chart*)	42
9	GERMANY: ZONES OF OCCUPATION, 1945	88
10	HITLER'S 'PEACEFUL AGGRESSIONS', 1933–39	92
11	GERMANY'S GREATEST MODERN EXPANSION, 1942	95
12	GERMANY BEFORE AND AFTER WORLD WAR I	98
13	BISMARCK'S UNITED GERMANY, 1871–1918	103
14	THE GERMAN *Bund* OF 1815	110
15–18	THE EXPANSION OF BRANDENBURG-PRUSSIA, 1415–1795	116–17
19	THE KINGDOM OF THE FRANKS	134
20	THE EMPIRE OF CHARLES THE GREAT	136
21	THE PARTITION OF VERDUN, A.D. 843	138

Maps 2, 3 and 4 are reproduced from *Germany: A General and Regional Geography*, by Robert E. Dickinson (Methuen & Co. Ltd.).

Maps 5 and 21 are reproduced from *A Geography of Europe*, edited by George W. Hoffmann (Copyright, 1953), by permission of the Ronald Press Company, New York.

Map 7 is reproduced from *The Shorter Cambridge Medieval History*, Vol. II, by the late C. W. Previté-Orton, by permission of Cambridge University Press.

Maps 19 and 20 are reproduced from *Der Grosse Herder*, by permission of Verlag Herder, Freiburg, as adapted by K. Reinhardt for his *Germany: 2000 Years* (Bruce Company, Milwaukee).

MAP I

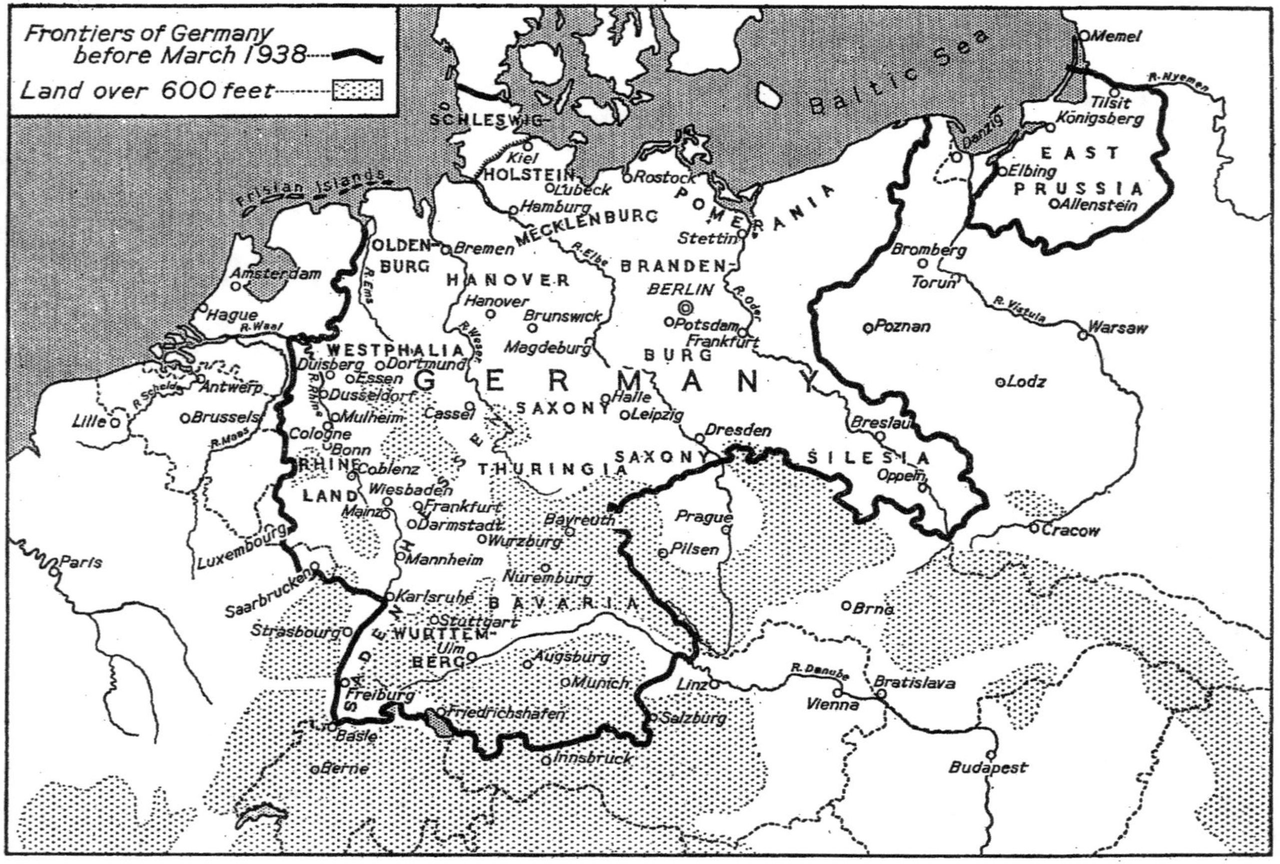
Frontiers of Germany before March 1938
Land over 600 feet
Baltic Sea
Frisian Islands
SCHLESWIG
HOLSTEIN
Kiel
Lübeck
Rostock
Hamburg
MECKLENBURG
POMERANIA
Stettin
OLDENBURG
Bremen
HANOVER
Hanover
Brunswick
BRANDENBURG
BERLIN
Potsdam
Frankfurt
Magdeburg
R. Elbe
R. Oder
R. Weser
R. Ems
WESTPHALIA
Duisberg
Dortmund
Essen
Dusseldorf
Mulheim
Cologne
Bonn
Coblenz
RHINELAND
R. Rhine
GERMANY
SAXONY
Halle
Leipzig
Dresden
Cassel
THURINGIA
SILESIA
Breslau
Oppeln
Wiesbaden
Mainz
Frankfurt
Darmstadt
Wurzburg
Bayreuth
Mannheim
Nuremburg
BAVARIA
Karlsruhe
Stuttgart
WURTTEMBERG
Ulm
Augsburg
Munich
Freiburg
Friedrichshafen
Basle
Berne
Innsbruck
Salzburg
Linz
Prague
Pilsen
Brno
Vienna
Bratislava
R. Danube
Budapest
Cracow
Lodz
Poznan
Warsaw
R. Vistula
Bromberg
Torun
Danzig
Elbing
Königsberg
Tilsit
Memel
R. Nyemen
EAST PRUSSIA
Allenstein
Amsterdam
Hague
R. Waal
Antwerp
R. Schelde
Brussels
R. Maas
Lille
Paris
Luxembourg
Saarbrucken
Strasbourg

Part I *The Peoples of Germany*

CHAPTER I

PREHISTORIC GERMANY

GERMANY'S first man (if this chinless creature can be called a man) of whom we have any knowledge, lived—or at any rate died—in the valley of the Neckar river near Heidelberg several hundred thousand years ago. We know nothing of his habits or of his way of life, whether he used tools or had fire, for *homo heidelbergensis* has left us only a portion of his skull: to wit, one lower jawbone. Some prefer to regard him as no more than a very highly developed ape, and he was certainly not a direct ancestor of modern man. Many ages later a creature with rather more of a chin and a larger brain capacity than *homo heidelbergensis* flourished in the valley of the Neander river near to Düsseldorf, and this *homo neanderthalensis* lived in caves, hunted animals with simple tools and made fires. Unlike Heidelberg Man (who is unique) Neanderthal Man seems to have been similar to beings living at approximately the same time in a number of other parts of Europe, where their skulls, and in several cases complete skeletons, have been found. Neanderthal Man of the old Stone Age was not yet *homo sapiens*, that first 'true man' who was the ancestor of us all, but this 'true man' was to appear soon afterwards (geologically speaking)—during the culmination of the fourth and last glacial period in Europe—on the inhospitable tundra or steppe which covered those parts of Europe not enveloped by the ice-sheets. His life must have been nasty, brutish and very cold, but the contraction of the ice-sheets was to change the climate of Europe from arctic to sub-arctic and then to bring forests and animals of a more temperate zone. Mesolithic (or middle Stone Age) man was the recipient of these blessings and many traces of this individual have been found in Germany. He occasionally forsook his nomadic habits and practised a primitive agriculture, he had learned to domesticate animals, he could build himself a crude shelter in which to live, his stone tools were more varied and better finished than those of Palaeolithic man and he could speak intelligibly to his fellows, though the art of writing was as yet unknown to him. Above all he could draw. While this Mesolithic man still flourished in the Danube and the Rhine valleys, and indeed over most of Europe, the great river valleys of the adjoining regions of north Africa and south-western Asia had passed out of pre-history into history. The civilizations of the Nile and the Euphrates valleys which came into existence at this time were literate and urban and their weapons and tools were no longer of stone only, but of bronze also. They were indeed two stages ahead of Europe (and particularly of north Germany, Denmark and south Sweden) where the Neolithic (or new Stone Age) culture was only slowly creeping up from the south.

Geographically considered Europe had by this time pretty well taken the shape it has retained through historical times. The land-bridges were down between the continent of Europe and North Africa, between Britain and Ireland and between Britain and the Continent; the Mediterranean had filled up to approximately its present shore-line; the Thames no longer flowed into the Rhine; the Baltic had become a sea and Denmark a peninsula. The dense forests that now covered most of this area had to be laboriously cleared by fire and by the polished stone axe (the most characteristic Neolithic tool and the most important) in order that man could settle down, as now at last he wanted to do, and till the soil in farmsteads and villages. A vigorous 'Danubian' culture spread at this time far beyond the Danube valley proper, through Moravia, Galicia and Poland as far as the Vistula in the east, and across Silesia, Saxony and Bavaria to the Rhineland in the west. The people of the second stage of this Danubian culture (from about 2500 to 2100 B.C.) built sturdy timber houses—remnants of which have been found in Swabia, for instance—and established contacts with Italy, Crete and Asia. These contacts helped to bring the Neolithic Age to an end, for by the third Danubian phase (2100 to 1700 B.C.) bronze implements and jewellery were being imported and a local copper industry had made its appearance. Farther north—in Thuringia, in Saxony and beyond—the stone battle-axe still reigned supreme (just as the European arctic still remained in the Stone Age when the rest of Europe was already using iron), for the metal cultures came to northern Europe by sea from the Mediterranean area or up the Danube valley from the south-east.

The new Bronze Age which now dawned witnessed the rise of the culture of the remarkable 'Beaker Folk', stretching from Spain to Poland. In this age the Danube valley traded extensively with western, eastern and northern Europe as well as developing further its contacts with the south. Europe was now one vast trading area, and copper and bronze articles from one end of the Continent found their way easily to the other. In central Germany a very prosperous era dawned, and its warrior chieftains were buried with great pomp, loaded with jewels and finely wrought weapons. The Bronze Age in Europe indeed culminated in the making of these tumuli, or burial mounds (about 1300 to 1000 B.C.).

Central Europe now passed to yet another level of material and cultural development with the coming of iron from north Italy—where the Iron Age had already commenced. The famous 'Hallstadt' culture (named from the finds at Hallstadt near Salzburg) saw bronze gradually supplanted by iron weapons and tools. By 650 B.C. the Age of Bronze was virtually over in the Danube valley. The Iron Age was essentially the period of Celtic domination over the greater part of Europe north of the Alps and south of the Baltic. The long iron or bronze swords of Hallstadt Age 'C' are found in south Germany and on the Swiss plateau, in Alsace, down the Rhine and in Burgundy, and even spread south-west into Spain, wielded by the Celtic warriors. A century or so later, in Hallstadt Age 'D' (around 500 B.C.) these warriors, armed with short iron swords, spread to the Lower Rhine and Meuse valleys, into northern and western France, to the Garonne and over the Pyrenees into Spain. Soon they were to penetrate into north Italy. These Celtic Iron Age peoples traded down the Rhine valley, through the port of Marseilles with southern Italy and Greece. By the fourth century B.C. the Celtic culture known as La Tène (from one of its settlements in Switzerland, near Neuchâtel) was spreading to central Germany. Gauls belonging to this highly developed culture sacked Rome itself in 386 B.C., and by 350 B.C. had occupied in north Italy what came to be called 'Cisalpine Gaul' by the Romans.

CHAPTER II

THE GERMANIC TRIBES

THE Germanic tribes first thrust themselves into history a century before the Christian era, when the Cimbri and the Teutoni invaded the provinces of Transalpine and Cisalpine Gaul of the Roman republic and were defeated and destroyed in two battles by the Roman general Marius. These two tribes passed out of history as quickly as they had entered it. Half a century later they were followed by other migrants. Their successors bore many different names, but by the end of the second century A.D. not one of the Germanic tribes that had harassed the Roman Empire during the days of Caesar, Augustus and their successors right up to the death of Marcus Aurelius (A.D. 180) remained a menace to it. Extermination, assimilation, expulsion or simply disappearance had removed them all. But unfortunately for the Empire a fresh and much more dangerous group of Germanic tribes now appeared—the Alemanni (or Suevi), the Franks, the Saxons, the Goths and others—and within the space of two more centuries they had literally hacked the Empire in the west into pieces.

The earlier Germanic tribes, against whom Julius Caesar and Drusus and Germanicus and Marcus Aurelius fought, and which were described by Tacitus and other writers, have only antiquarian interest to the student of the history of Germany. There is even some doubt as to whether all of them were strictly 'Germanic', for some of their leaders bore Celtic names and there was a tendency among the Gauls of what is now France to describe all peoples who came from across the Rhine or who lived beyond its farther bank as 'Germans'. The whole of the south of the modern area of Germany was probably occupied up to the second century B.C. by Celtic peoples, and a certain admixture was inevitable as the Germanic invaders from the area of the lower Elbe and the Danish peninsula pushed them southward and westward and occupied their lands. Modern German scholars have shown a tendency to characterize any tribe or tribal leader defeated on the field of battle by the Romans as 'Celtic' and any that won a victory or victories over the Romans as 'Germanic'. No French scholar has retaliated to the extent of claiming that the national hero of modern Germans, Hermann (or Arminius), who destroyed the three legions of Varus in A.D. 9, was really a Celt, though one, after pointing out that Gaul was only saved from a Germanic invasion by the invasion of Julius Caesar over Ariovistus near Strassbourg in 58 B.C., and regretting that having thus saved it he was immediately to turn and reduce all Gaul to vassalage, mordantly remarks that, anyway, a Roman conquest of Gaul was preferable to a Germanic one.

The Franks, the Burgundians, the Lombards and the Goths constituted the main divisions of those Germanic tribes which between the second and the sixth centuries A.D. swarmed out of Scandinavia and the Danish peninsula and the lower Elbe—lands across the whole of central Europe, and also in some cases into the Balkans, into Italy and into Iberia. (At the same time tribes closely related to these were invading the islands of Britain, but with them we are not concerned here.) Out of the tribes of the great *Völkerwanderung* (as this movement of peoples has come to be called by German writers and their imitators) and of their intermingling with the peoples and the civilization they found in the new lands they occupied, have emerged the countries and states of western Europe as we have come to know them in modern times.

The Franks eventually moved their centre of power too far to the west (into France), the Lombards too far to the south (into Italy) and the Visigoths too far west (into Spain) for their subsequent history to belong to that of Germany, but the tribes that remained in Central Europe—the Bavarians, the Saxons, the Swabians (or Allemanians), the Franconians and the Lorrainers—as they gradually came to be called when tribal duchies bearing these names came into existence—were the first recognizably direct ancestors of the west and south Germans of today. Those regions known as 'Bavaria' and 'Franconia', for instance, have had a continuous thread of political and ethnic development, as such, ever since the break-up of the Empire of Charles the Great at the Partition of Verdun (A.D. 843). It was about this time that they really changed (though the change was subtle and almost unremarked until long afterwards) from being just some of the Germanic tribes into being the truly *German* tribes. Their language was now sufficiently different from the latinized tongue of the west Franks for the Treaty of Verdun to need to be drawn up not only in the west Frankish language (which was eventually to develop into French) but also in the *lingua theodisca* or popular tongue of the German tribes—and 'theodisca' was to become, in the vernacular, 'deutsch'. From some points of view, therefore, the history of Germany does not really begin

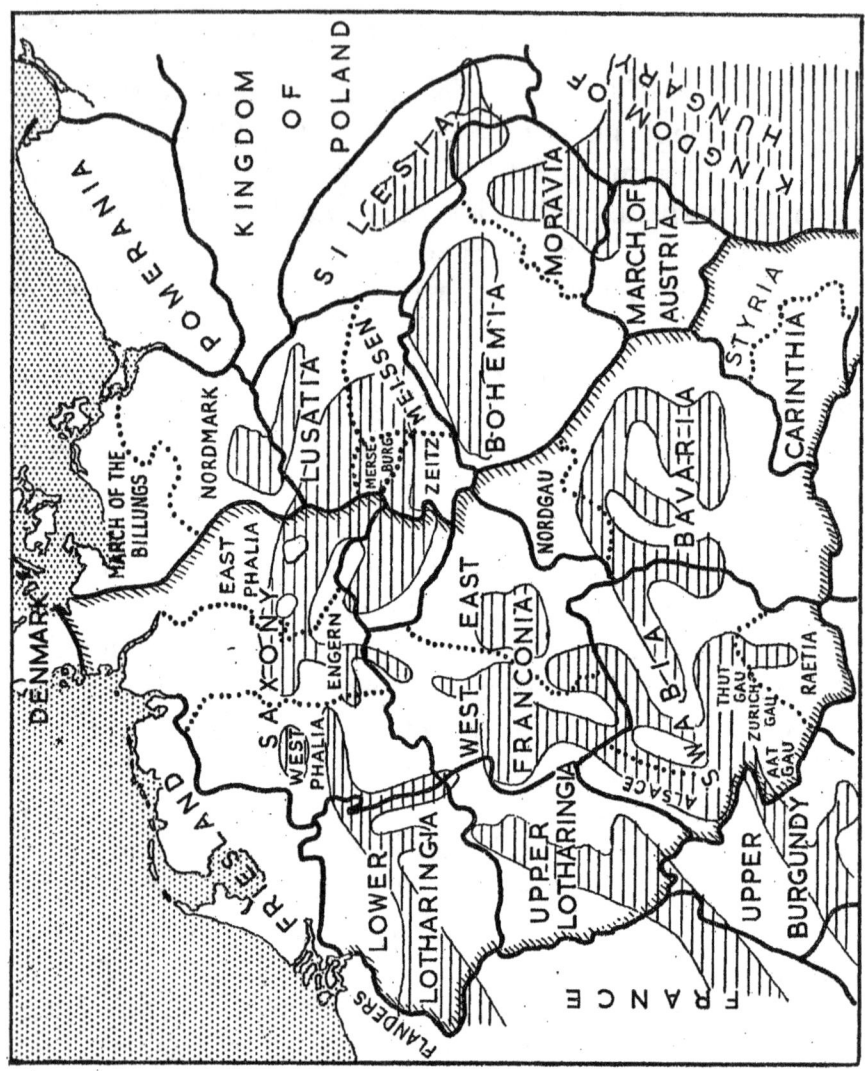

MAP 2. TRIBAL DUCHIES AND MARCHES OF THE GERMAN LANDS, A.D. 950–1250

(Forest-free land shaded)
—*after Dickinson*

until after the Partition of Verdun, and even then it was to be no more for a long time to come than the histories of these separate German tribes as they lived in their independent or nearly independent duchies. The Carolingian Empire, though an extremely interesting experiment in the unification of the continental peoples of western Europe (under an emperor who called himself 'Roman' but never either 'German' or 'French'), no more belongs to the history of Germany than does its predecessor the much more limited and unambitious Merovingian Empire, and it is a misreading of history to treat it as such.[1]

It is thus only by a stretch of the imagination (but one of which many Germans have found themselves capable) that Charles the Great can be treated as a German king or a German hero at all, and only by an even wilder one that leaders of the *Völkerwanderung* such as Alaric, and Theodoric the Ostrogoth, and the other historical figures presented in a somewhat confused way in the twelfth-century German epic poem, the *Niebelungenlied*, can be claimed as such. As for Wotan and the other Wagnerian gods and heroes, they belong to a remote Norse mythology to which the Germans have no exclusive claim at all, but must share with the Scandinavians, the Anglo-Saxons and all other peoples possessing or sharing 'Germanic' origins. The fact that Vercingetorix lived in Gaul (some of which is now part of modern France), and fought against the Romans, does not make a Frenchman of him, and he is not claimed as such by moderate-minded Frenchmen today—though one French writer, perhaps with pardonable pride, does refer to him as 'notre Vercingetorix'. It is no more logical to regard Arminius, who lived in what Tacitus and Caesar called

[1] See further pp. 133-38.

'Germania' (and some of which is now modern Germany) and also fought against the Romans, as a German in the sense of being the fellow countryman of Bismarck the Prussian Junker. That the *Chanson de Roland*, written in French, and the *Rolandslied*, written in German (in the twelfth century), both commemorate the same hero, Roland, the Carolingian general who died at Roncevalles, points to the fact that he and his exploits belong to the common western European heritage of the French *and* the German peoples, and the attempt of either to stake an exclusive claim to him is merely illustrative of the mental excesses to which the very modern sentiment of nationalism can lead. It is undoubtedly true that 'Charlemagne' will continue to figure in histories of France and 'Karl der Grosse' in histories of Germany, and rightly so if he is treated in proper perspective. He belongs to the prehistory (in the German sense of *Ur-Geschichte*) of both France and Germany—and perhaps of Italy as well—because in his time those lands had as yet no separate and distinct historical development.

CHAPTER III

THE TRIBAL REGIONS

THE seven tribal regions of Bavaria, Swabia (or Allemannia), Thuringia, Franconia, Saxony, Lorraine and Friesland[1] had virtually nothing in common politically, and no sense of cohesion at all, when they found themselves linked together as a separate kingdom under one Frankish king, Louis (called 'The German') in A.D. 840. But they became rapidly so used to being together under the same rule that, after the Carolingian Empire had disappeared, and Frankish domination had ceased in Germany, they voluntarily agreed to elect a common king from among the rulers of the tribal groups. Thus in the year A.D. 911 the Duke of Franconia became the first truly 'German' king, chosen by the Germans themselves and not simply imposed upon them. This free choice had an element of stability in it that the purely arbitrary partitions of the later Carolingians had lacked. Conrad I, and his much more powerful successor Henry the Fowler, Duke of Saxony (A.D. 918), were indigenous German princes in a sense and to an extent that no Carolingian, even Charles the Great himself, had ever been.

These seven tribal regions became seven duchies which preserved their cultural if not always their political individuality right through the Middle Ages, and which

[1] See map on p. 8. Friesland and Thuringia are sometimes excluded because they did not become independent tribal duchies.

did not split up politically to an irreparable extent until that anarchic period of the thirteenth century which followed the ending of the Hohenstauffen line of emperors. It must be remembered of course that in the tenth century, and indeed until much later, the well-populated areas which formed the core of each duchy tended to be separated by fringes of under-populated or even unpopulated land—forest, mountain or swamp—to a much greater extent than, say, the different duchies and provinces of France or the shires (or even the former kingdoms of the Heptarchy) in England. The ruler of one German duchy might conquer another (as Henry of Saxony did Lorraine in A.D. 925) and attach it to his dominions, but that did not mean—even if the conquest was permanent, and often it was not—that the cultural individuality of the inhabitants of the two duchies would be merged. Very often the ordinary inhabitant of one tribal region would not even be aware of, or at least not affected in any way by, the ruler of another becoming his overlord. Thus when the Franks drove a huge wedge between the Saxons (to the north) and the Swabians and Bavarians (to the south) when they conquered and colonized the upper Main valley and took over a large part of Thuringia, the local and tribal culture of Thuringia was not extinguished, but continued to flourish and has to a large extent persisted into modern times.

It mattered even to a lesser extent in the development of the separate tribal duchies, whether a Saxon or a Salian or a Hohenstauffen emperor was elected by their dukes to the ultimate overlordship of all Germany, or whether his family came from the north or the west or the south. It mattered a great deal of course whether he was a strong or a weak ruler, what his relations with the Church and the Papacy were, whether he had personal or dynastic ambitions abroad, and whether he wanted to embark on a crusade or not.

Had the fortunes of Germany run more parallel to those of France and England during the later Middle Ages it is probable that these tribal duchies would have grown closer and closer together in cultural development and political interest as population in the sparsely inhabited areas and as trade between them increased, and that eventually a unified and stable 'German' kingdom with one ruler and one central administration, possessing real authority through its length and breadth, might have emerged long before the modern period began. Under the Salian Emperor Henry IV, indeed, the consolidation of Germany was, up to the year A.D. 1076, more complete than that of either England (the Oath of Salisbury had yet to be sworn) or of France at that same date.

But the tide of history was to run the other way for Germany from the end of the eleventh century onwards. The tribal dukes each preserved his autonomy under the Salian emperors as they had under the Saxon kings and emperors, and most of the Salian emperors managed to underline the existence of a *regnum teutonicum*, or state of Germany, without having to assail this autonomy. But the continued attacks of the Papacy on the authority of the emperors in Germany (notably those of Gregory VII and Innocent III) and the extent to which the Hohenstauffens allowed the disintegrating forces of territorial feudalism to grow in Germany while they were engaged elsewhere, broke down the sense of 'belonging together' that had been developing among the German peoples and their rulers ever since the tenth (or even the ninth) century, and led to the setting up of a whole series of petty 'states within the state' in the thirteenth century.

The thirteenth century indeed saw the dissolution of

the old 'German State' that Henry the Fowler and the Ottos had created out of the eastern division of the Empire of Charlemagne, and by then the old tribal duchies no longer existed in any political sense. Their traditional frontiers had disappeared through partition after partition. Swabia was the last to preserve its integrity, but by A.D. 1250 it too had broken up, and into even smaller fragments than some of the others. A mass of dukes, margraves, counts, bishops, urban oligarchies and imperial knights, each maintaining his or its own petty despotism over, often, only a few square miles of territory, had taken their place. Larger dukedoms and principalities still existed (and indeed still remained to be founded) beyond the Elbe, where a system of territorial marches was pushing German colonization eastwards, but western and to a large extent central Germany—the Germany of the seven tribal duchies— was now hopelessly divided and subdivided. 'The German state' had to be refounded in the late thirteenth century on a smaller scale and the cohesive authority of the Holy Roman Emperor over it was never again to be more than nominal. The Golden Bull (A.D. 1356) confirmed the trend of the century that had then elapsed since the death of the Emperor Frederick II, and the growth of 'modern' concepts of sovereignty from that time onwards were to hasten the process. After the Reformation these hundreds of German statelets were no longer even to belong to one universal Church, or the rulers of many of them to recognize the authority of the Pope, but for two (if not three) hundred years before that time they had barely recognized that of the Emperor. For centuries after the year 1250, claims Haller, German history lacked all broad significance, and from the thirteenth to the fifteenth had really no unity at all.

CHAPTER IV

NORTHERNERS AND SOUTHERNERS

AS late as the second century B.C. Celtic tribes occupied the whole of the southern half of what is now Germany (Hessen, Baden, Württemberg, Thuringia and Saxony) and also the lands which became Austria and Bohemia. They were then subjected to attack from the south and west by the Romans from across the Alps and the Rhine on the one side, and by Germanic tribes from the north and east on the other. The Alpine stock of which they principally consisted was thus subjected to dilution by a Nordic and by a Mediterranean influx at one and the same time, so that by the time of the break-up of the Roman Empire and the abandonment of its *limes* (or frontier defences) along the Rhine, Main and Danube and of all its provinces east of the Rhine, the inhabitants of southern Germany had become very mixed indeed. To a lesser extent (for the Celtic hold on that area had long since been loosened) the same was happening in the northern half of Germany as well. The breakdown of the old 'frontier' between Celts and Germanic peoples under this dual pressure, and the disappearance of a distinctively Celtic culture in south Germany early in the Christian era, makes it difficult for any period since then to draw any satisfactory line between 'south' and 'north' Germans. The antagonisms and the differences between 'east' and 'west' Germans, on the other hand, became much more important historically as time went on.

MAP 3. THE DISTRIBUTION OF GERMAN DIALECTS
—after Dickinson

Low German dialects—
Shaded diagonally left to right

Middle German dialects—
Shaded vertically

High German dialects—
Shaded diagonally right to left

Non-German—
White

Mixed German and Non-German—
Broken lines

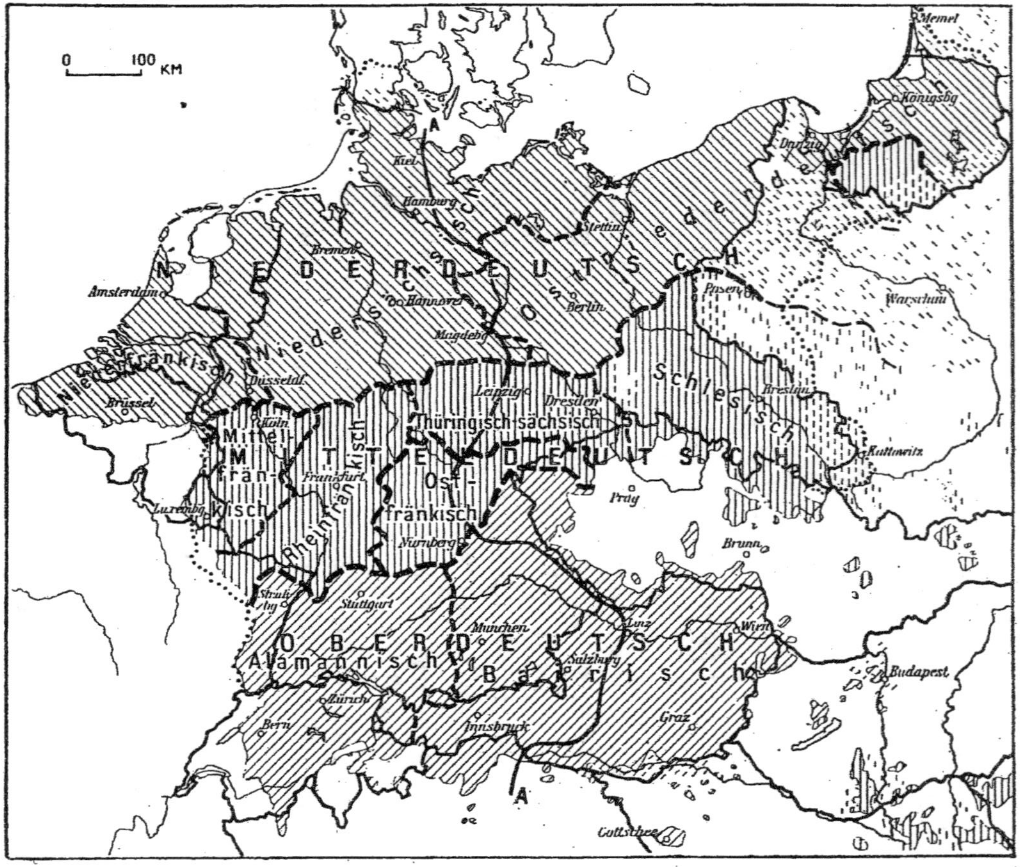

Even the linguistic difference between northern and southern Germany that developed around A.D. 500 when 'Low' and 'High' German began to be clearly distinguishable one from another (and when the second sound-shift took place in the latter), did not prove enough to set up a clear line of demarkation between the cultures of the south and the north. Both were converted to Christianity at the same time; both absorbed similar elements of the old Roman civilization; both received the same sorts of feudalism; both (with purely local variations) practised the same types of agriculture.

It was possible to distinguish a Franconian from a Frisian, a Bavarian from a Lorrainer, a Swabian from a Saxon, but no more easily than a Swabian from a Bavarian or a Frisian from a Saxon, by the time of the high Middle Ages. Terms used to describe a people of north Germany even came to be applied to those of a south German area as well, so that the early medieval description 'Saxon' (meaning an inhabitant of Westphalia or Eastphalia, living in what we now call Lower Saxony) came to be applied before the end of the medieval period to the people living in the new-won lands on the upper Elbe in the angle between Thuringia and Bohemia, in the area that was to become the modern state and kingdom of Saxony with its capital at Dresden.

Only very much later, in early modern times, when the peoples of the North German plain tended to embrace Protestantism more readily and those south of the river Main to remain Catholic, did more fundamental differences begin to emerge between south and north Germans, and even then almost the whole of the valley of the Rhine, from the Swiss to the Netherlands border, remained Catholic, with very close cultural ties throughout its length, so that a man from Cologne or Aachen, while he was of course different from a man from Freiburg or Heidelberg did not feel the other to be a 'foreigner' in the way he thought a Pomeranian or an east Prussian to be something alien and different.

This lack of fundamental distinction or difference from the early Middle Ages onwards between the peoples of south and of north Germany, west of the Elbe-Saale line at least, was to be an important factor in German history. It became progressively more difficult to stir them up against each other, and their common anti-French and anti-Habsburg feeling became stronger as the French and the Habsburg monarchies consolidated and expanded and began to interfere more and more in the internal affairs of the various German states. These states (many of which were forced to accept the 'protection' of Napoleonic France for a time) were nevertheless very suspicious of the new (and barely German) power of Brandenburg-Prussia which arose to the north and east of them from the sixteenth century onwards, and were not prepared to accept Prussian leadership of a united Germany until a full two generations after Prussia had come into possession of the Rhine provinces, and had inherited Austria's role of protector of the Rhine frontier and of the German lands west of the Rhine against France. Once the need for this leadership had been brought home to western Germany as a whole (and it was a conclusion that was reached reluctantly, and only after the bitterness of 1848 and of 1866), all parts of it, both south and north, co-operated in the Bismarckian-Hohenzollern Empire. That some of the northern states (such as Hanover) were annexed by Prussia, but the southern states taken into partnership by her on specially favourable terms, was less a reflection of the differences between south and north than of Bismarck's assessment of the relative strength, and relative menace to Prussia's ambitions in Germany, of the particularism of the northern and the southern states. Frankfurt-am-Main, a border city between north and south, was annexed more because it had been a hotbed of radicalism, had a sturdily independent financial and commercial policy not always in accord with Prussia's, and was (as the capital of the old *Bund*) a symbol of Austrian leadership in Germany under which Bismarck had spent several frustrated years as Prussian delegate to the *Bundestag*. Baden, on the other hand, which had been the centre of the radical-nationalist and parliamentary party before 1848 and had witnessed two attempts to establish a republic on its soil during the years of revolution, was not annexed. In 1866 it would have affronted not only France, but also the Papacy and the Swiss, for Prussia to annex Baden. Nobody but Britain (and that for sentimental rather than practical reasons) cared very much about the annexation of a Protestant, politically reactionary and socially backward Hanover, separating the main territory of Prussia from her Rhine province and constituting a definite strategic menace to her when siding (as it did) with Prussia's rivals, the Habsburgs.

It has been necessary to swing the telescope over a wide horizon, all the way from the Celts of the Hallstadt culture to the Second Reich of Bismarck to make the simple point about the lack of fundamental differences or rivalries between northerners and southerners living in Germany west of the Elbe. It will be far easier to define the differences between east and west Germans.

CHAPTER V

EASTERNERS AND WESTERNERS

THE historical as well as the geographical dividing line between eastern and western Germany is the river Elbe in its lower and middle course, from its mouth just north of the city of Hamburg, down to just south of Magdeburg, whence the line continues along its tributary the river Saale to the source of that river near Eger in the Fichtel-Gebirge. From the nearby source of the southward flowing river Naab, also in the Fichtel-Gebirge only a few miles away (the river Main, flowing westward, rises there too), the line continues on to where the river Naab flows into the Danube just above Regensburg, then turns south-eastwards and follows the river Danube itself until it reaches the Hungarian plain at Bratislava—a 'frontier town' between the Germans (who called it Pressburg), the Slovaks (to whom it is Bratislava) and the Magyars (who knew it as Poszony).

Now, since the rivers Elbe and Danube run generally from south-east to north-west along the portions of their course just defined, and only the minor rivers Saale and Naab (which complete this 'line of demarkation') flow anything like approximating to south and north, the distinction that can be drawn between 'east' and 'west' Germans, on the basis of this line, is slightly imprecise; but it is nevertheless a very useful one, and has, as has been indicated, great historical significance. Not only does it roughly correspond with the eastern boundary of

MAP 4. GERMAN MEDIEVAL BISHOPRICS (ABOUT A.D. 1000)
—*after Dickinson*

(*Note* that nearly all are west of the river Elbe)

the Empire of Charlemagne (and of the more strictly 'German' Empire of Henry the Fowler, Otto the Great and their successors), but it also approximates remarkably closely to the line of the 'iron curtain'[1] between the 'east' and 'west' Germanies of today.

Those parts of Germany which had been part of the Carolingian Empire remained 'western', but the rest remained 'eastern' in more ways than one, and some parts of the latter were, in the course of the centuries, conquered or reconquered from time to time by non-German peoples and powers. One such recession came during the latter half of the tenth century, in the reign of Otto II (when the Slavs between the Elbe and the Oder successfully rebelled against the Emperor), and another and bigger retreat, from a more advanced salient, followed in the fifteenth century when the power of the Teutonic Knights collapsed after their defeat at Tannenberg (A.D. 1410). This relative instability of Germany's eastern frontier (although the boundary of the Holy Roman Empire on the east did not change appreciably after the fourteenth century—for the lands of the Teutonic Knights were never formally incorporated within the Empire) meant that an already mixed population, of which the Germans were in places little more than a ruling caste, became more and more mixed as time went on. The inhabitants of Prussia, for instance, when that state became a power to be reckoned with in the seventeenth century, were never more than very partially Germanic in their ultimate origins, though by modern times they were definitely German in speech and culture. Only a very small area of the Brandenburg section of Prussia lay west of the line of the Elbe, while much of it lay east of the Oder. The whole of east

[1] Compare maps on p. 26 and p. 88.

Prussia, of course, was east of the Vistula. It was a quite pardonable exaggeration for west Germans to regard the Prussians as simply Slavs with but a thin veneer of Germanic culture, and many of them did so.

The expansion of the Empire to absorb Silesia, Bohemia and Moravia (in addition to Brandenburg and Pomerania farther north) between the days of Henry the Fowler and those of Frederick Barbarossa, added of course to that Empire yet another great belt of territory inhabited by Slavs rather than Germans, another area, incidentally, which it found impossible permanently to absorb, least of all to Germanize.

In the west the situation was very different. The Franks indeed became so very 'western' in attitude that, although they were as Germanic in origin as any of the tribes, they ceased to be German in feeling and in culture and let themselves—like their neighbours the Norsemen in Normandy—become entirely latinized, adopting the French language, and emerging from the era of partitions in which the Carolingian Empire dissolved as the core of 'the French people'. The other west Germans—the Frisians, the Swabians (even the borderland Lorrainers) and others—did not go so far as this, but although they maintained their German speech and ways, they too became the protagonists of what they understood to be the Roman civilization, its staunch defenders and its buffer against the Slavs. Slav expansion westwards from the sixth century onwards had for a time endangered the very existence of the Germanic tribes, but the counter-attack of the Carolingians in the seventh century and the much more decisive ones of the German emperors and their frontier margraves from the eleventh century onwards, won back the lost ground for several centuries, though much of it was subsequently to be lost again, so that the Germans today find themselves with an eastern frontier against the Slavs rather less favourable than that which Henry the Fowler bequeathed to them on his death over a thousand years ago.

In this process, and in the midst of this insecurity lasting a full millenium, the east Germans have developed characteristics in many ways differing from those of the west Germans, and these differences remain. There is a cultural line of demarkation between west and east (very roughly at the line of the Elbe) such as has never developed in Germany between the south and the north.

CHAPTER VI
GERMANS *VERSUS* SLAVS

FROM just before the beginning of the Christian era it was the Germanic tribes who exerted pressure upon the Celtic culture of western Europe and upon the boundaries of the still-expanding Roman Republic and Empire, but even before their onslaughts had brought about the complete disintegration of that Empire, they were themselves assailed from behind by even fiercer and more barbaric invaders. They succeeded in repulsing the short and sharp attack of the Huns in the fourth century, and the more sustained, but no less menacing incursions of the Avars in the sixth and the Magyars in the tenth century. Otto the Great's victory over the Magyars at Lechfeld[1] in A.D. 955 was a great landmark in the establishment of the eastern frontiers of Germany, for although the Magyars settled permanently and founded a kingdom in the nearby Hungarian plain of the middle Danube valley, they never again threatened the Upper Danube or the Rhine valleys. The March or border province of Austria was established by the Empire as a 'buffer state' between the land of the Bavarians and the Magyars, and was never wholly lost, even when the Ottoman Turks came up out of Asia Minor and, in the fifteenth century, conquered the Magyars and captured Vienna, the chief city of Austria. The Turks were brought to a halt in Styria, where to this day can be

[1] In Bavaria.

MAP 5. GERMANY'S EASTERN MARCHES—*after Hoffman*

found adjacent villages, a mile or so apart, the one bearing many traces of Turkish occupation and the other none at all.

The Magyars (and later the Turks) thrust themselves like a great wedge between the northern and the southern Slavs who had come out of Asia to close in behind the Germanic tribes as these moved westwards into the outlying provinces of the Roman Empire. Sometimes (and notably in the Balkan peninsula) the Slavs advanced far enough to occupy genuinely 'Roman' soil, but north of the Alps they were stopped before they reached the line of the Elbe-Saale-Naab-Danube. Just as their greatest failure was their inability to occupy and colonize the fertile plain of Hungary, their greatest success was their permanent settlement of the 'salient' of Bohemia and Moravia, protected towards the south, the west and the north by a mountain wall, which formed three sides of a square. North of this salient, with its natural boundaries, the Poles found it much harder to establish, in the plains, a stable frontier with the Germans, though they founded a great and powerful kingdom, while the Slavs along the shores of the Baltic never did manage to compress the Germans for any length of time. By conquest, colonization, and conversion, by trade, by cultural penetration, and finally (in recent times) by 'fifth column' techniques, the Germans kept thrusting a thick finger along the Baltic, as far as Esthonia. Even when the Battle of Tannenberg and the Peace of Thorn (A.D. 1455) lost them their political control there in the fifteenth century, they left behind them thousands of colonists to continue the cultural struggle. It was a warped and fanatical member of one of these 'Baltic' German families, Alfred Rosenberg, who was to direct Adolf Hitler's attempt first (in 1939-40) to withdraw all German colonists from the 'Baltic States', and then (in 1941-44) to re-settle them there and re-incorporate the Baltic littoral in a greater German Reich, thus avenging, five hundred years later, the humiliation of Tannenberg.

If the Germans succeeded in digging a finger into Slavonic Europe along the southern shores of the Baltic, the Czechs of Bohemia managed to shake a fist in the faces of the Germans in the heart of central Europe. In a dim and distant past that has left no recorded history, but of which archaeology and philology tell the story, the Slavs had pushed the Germans out of Bohemia and Moravia into Bavaria, the name of which—the land of the *Baju-Wari* (the Marcomanni of the Romans)—itself enshrines evidence of this enforced migration. For this they have never been forgiven. A German may hate the Poles, but his hatred is (however unjustifiably) mixed with contempt. When Adolf Hitler made his Victory Speech after the defeat of Poland in 1939 he said of the Polish Army, 'Their organization was ... [pause] *Polish*' [with great emphasis], amid loud guffaws from his Nazi audience. A Czech may be hated just as much, but that hate is mixed with respect. When Hitler again made his notorious 'Ich oder Beneš' speech in September 1938, he paid President Beneš the tribute of treating him as a diabolically clever schemer, whom Europe was not large enough to hold with Hitler himself there too. He never called Beneš a fool or cast reflections on the skill or the courage of the Czechs.

But whether it was mixed with respect or contempt, the German hatred of the Slavs and their fear of them, is a legacy of the days of the *Völkerwanderung* and of the early Middle Ages which the events of recent centuries have done nothing to eradicate. It is a factor in German history and in the make-up of the German people that time seems to exacerbate rather than to abate.

The new kingdoms of Bohemia and of Poland, consolidating their power in the later Middle Ages, put a stop to further German expansion eastwards until they fell into decay in the seventeenth and eighteenth centuries. Then, with great satisfaction and without thought of mercy, the Germans collaborated with their other ill-wishers to wipe them off the map of Europe. Yet Poland and Bohemia had shared a common Catholic Christianity with Germany, going their separate ways in and after the Reformation as did the states of the Empire itself.

Perhaps the Germans would have succeeded better in their task of enveloping and assimilating the Poles and the Czechs had not Slavonic Europe developed a defence in depth through the rise of another and even greater Slavonic state farther east. This was Russia, unimportant before the sixteenth century, and not really a great power until the eighteenth had seen the eclipse of Sweden. The Grand Duchy of Muscovy had been no real menace to the Germans of the Empire, with whom it traded and exchanged ambassadors, for their mutual ambitions were so far heavily insulated from each other by intervening states—such as Sweden, Poland, Bohemia and Hungary. But there were inherent reasons why, when the insulation wore thin, Germany and Russia should become rivals. The Germans regarded themselves, through the Holy Roman emperors, as the true heirs to the Roman tradition; the Russians, with their Tsar and their orthodox faith, saw themselves as the heirs to Byzantium. The fall of Constantinople to the Ottoman Turks in the year A.D. 1453 had reinforced them in this belief. For a time the realities of the German-Russian rivalry were masked by the Turkish menace, against which they could from time to time assume they were conducting a common crusade, but their formal alliances even in this 'good cause' were few, and when that last crusader, John Sobieski (who was a Pole), had disappeared from the scene after saving Vienna in A.D. 1686 and the Turkish menace itself began to recede rapidly, their antagonism became open. Reasons of state still continued to draw them together in alliance from time to time (against Napoleon for instance, and in Bismarck's uneasy 'Triple Alliance' of the three emperors of Germany, Austria and Russia, or in the short-lived Hitler-Stalin Pact of 1939), but apart from such interludes their rivalry grew ever more deadly. Germany all but destroyed Russia in 1918 and again in 1941. In 1945 it was Russia's turn to rend Germany.

Yet the German-Slav rivalry was implacable even before Russia's intervention, and Germans still dislike Czechs and Poles more than they do Russians. A Czech who collaborates with the Germans is regarded as a traitor to his people and so is a German who collaborates with the Czechs. A Hitler-Beneš pact in 1939 or any other date was unthinkable, but most Germans thought Hitler very clever (as of course he was) to make one with Stalin in 1939, for it averted another simultaneous two-front war against France and Russia and left them to be dealt with piecemeal.

CHAPTER VII

GERMANS *VERSUS* LATINS

CHARLES the Great, as has been seen, ruled over an Empire that comprehended both modern Germany and modern France and in his day the German and the French people were not yet clearly differentiated one from another. Less than a century later, the Partition of Verdun (A.D. 843), followed by the disappearance of the 'Middle Kingdom' of Lotharingia (870) and by the extinction of the Carolingian Empire (889), had resulted in the territories which approximated to the Germany and the France of modern times drawing apart from each other in historical and linguistic development while sharing a common frontier. All traces and all memory of Lotharingia did not disappear immediately and the late medieval independent Duchy of Burgundy[1] represented a revival on a much more restricted geographical scale of the Lotharingian realm. Other inhabitants of 'Lotharingia' were eventually to assert their independence of both France and Germany—the Swiss in the thirteenth and the Netherlanders in the sixteenth century, for instance—and certain other border territories (such as Alsace and Lorraine) were to change hands, from the one to the other, several times: back, forth, and back again even within the last hundred years.

But while the borderlands remained in a state of

[1] Not to be confused with the *kingdom* of Burgundy (or Arles) located in the lower Rhône valley.

flux, the states and peoples of France and Germany crystallized very rapidly. In France this led to an ever-increasing authority and unity under the Capetian and Valois kings, but in Germany the crystallization was around smaller political nuclei within an equally definite common cultural sphere to that of France.

The clash of these two cultures along a disputed political frontier produced the great rivalry between Latin and German which still persists, even though it has recently become less significant than that between German and Slav. By the year A.D. 918 the tribal duchies on what was now the 'German' side of this boundary had accepted the suzerainty of a definitely German king (Henry the Fowler, Duke of Saxony). It was not until A.D. 987 that Hugh Capet gave a similar degree of stability to the infant kingdom of France. It was to be another two centuries before a serious clash between these two newly differentiated kingdoms (growing more and more apart all the time, despite their common Carolingian background and their common religion), for both were more than fully occupied either with internal consolidation or with attempts to expand in directions away from each other—the Capetian kings of France against the power of Normandy (from A.D. 1066 powerfully linked with England under a common ruler) to the west of them, and the German emperors (as they became in A.D. 962) southwards in their efforts to have and to hold Italy and eastwards across the Elbe against the Slavs. In addition, the Duchy of Burgundy acted as a buffer state between the two greater realms, attracting like a lightning conductor the animosity of each in turn. But from about A.D. 1270 onwards the antagonism between France and Germany grew more positive, as French expansive ambitions turned eastwards as well as west and southwards.

A period of more intense rivalry lasted until A.D. 1346, when France found herself distracted by the Hundred Years War against England. A century later the ambitions of France had crystallized (A.D. 1444) into a claim to all of what was called 'the Kingdom of Gaul', and the break-up of the power of Burgundy (at the Battle of Nancy, A.D. 1477) allowed the French king to seize most of the territory that was by now in dispute between Germany and France. The marriage of the Burgundian heiress, Mary (daughter of Charles the Bold, who was killed at Nancy), to the heir to the Habsburg realm, Maximilian, made the Habsburg dynasty (which had by now secured itself an almost automatic right to election as Holy Roman emperors) the protector and champion of Germany against further French encroachments for nearly three centuries—until the diplomatic revolution of 1756. Even then the rivalry did not cease, for a new champion of Germany's rights and claims was arising in the shape of Prussia. It was Prussia that was to lead Germany in successive humiliations of France, on the field of battle and around the council table, during the nineteenth century . . . and after.

CHAPTER VIII

GERMAN EXPANSION IN EUROPE

BEFORE the emergence of a distinguishably 'German' people in their tribal duchies it was impossible to differentiate 'German' from 'non-German' groups in the population of Europe. A case to point is that of the Frankish lands, which, under the Merovingian and Carolingian emperors, stretched westwards over much of what is now France and eastwards up the Main valley as far as Thuringia. But by the ninth century (the age of partitions) the east Franks had become the Germans of 'Franconia' and the west Franks the French of France. The Duchy of Lotharingia or Lorraine, lying between the lands of the east and the west Franks, thus came to be a borderland between France and Germany; the people of its western parts gradually gravitating towards a French overlordship, and of its eastern section[1] (nearest to the Rhine) toward a German affiliation, though this was a long process and nearly all of both upper and lower Lorraine remained for many centuries within the nominal boundaries of the Holy Roman Empire. The break-up of the Duchy of Burgundy at the beginning of modern times was to drive the frontiers of the German Empire back to approximately half-way between the Meuse and the Rhine rivers in their middle courses (which was approximately where the language boundary between French and German had also crystallized) and to give to

[1] See map on p. 8.

the French kings the ambition of obtaining the 'natural frontier' of the Rhine; but linguistically and culturally the boundary was by then firmly fixed, and political control rather than cultural absorption was all that was possible across the ethnic and linguistic frontier in and after the sixteenth century. When France possessed Alsace, for instance, those of its inhabitants who spoke German as their first language and considered themselves German by culture, continued as such, and when Germany possessed that province (as between 1871 and 1918), those who considered themselves French remained so. One eminent French politician of our own day was born a German subject in Alsace and did his military service in the German Army before 1914, but nobody has ever doubted that he is a Frenchman rather than a German, and it is inconceivable that he should have become German Foreign Minister after the Second World War. Nevertheless, other Alsatians, feeling themselves 'German' rather than 'French' have served Germany just as loyally as M. Schuman has served France.

The non-existence of a middle kingdom, on a scale comparable to Lotharingia, to the east of Germany, to cushion the contacts between Germans and Slavs and to give to the inhabitants a tradition of 'separateness'—such as the Dutch and the Swiss were to maintain and exploit—meant that things developed there through the centuries very differently from the way in which they did in the west. When the Saxons, who had been Christianized by missionaries out of Western Europe (and conquered temporarily by the Frankish rulers of the Carolingian Empire) themselves set out, as the new leaders of post-partition Germany, to conquer and convert the tribes to the east of the Elbe, they did not at first encounter people on a comparable level of civilization to themselves. Consequently, the primitive Wends and the Sorbs, immediately east of the lower and middle Elbe, were rapidly Germanized, soon forgetting their Slav origins and becoming indistinguishable from other Germans. A second phase of German expansion eastwards found the Slavs across the Oder and upper Elbe rivers tougher nuts to crack than the people of Holstein, Mecklenburg and Brandenburg (to give these areas their modern names) had been. In Pomerania, Silesia and on the mountain borders of Bohemia (again to use the modern names) German colonization took place in the midst of a Slav population which retained its cultural individuality and language, and very often remained under Slav rulers. Up to the fourteenth century this peaceful penetration produced as near to a true 'partnership' of German and Slav as has ever occurred, and even when the new and powerful Slav states of Poland and Bohemia (and the Magyar state of Hungary) had produced their own civilizations and had developed powers capable of dealing with Germans on equal terms, the sterling qualities and the many skills of the Germans, in agriculture, mining, town-building and so on, made them welcome as individual or group settlers in these Slav kingdoms, if only they were prepared to become subjects of Slavonic rulers. German 'Nationalism' in its aggressive modern sense not yet having developed (its first real manifestation only came in the fifteenth century), they were usually very happy to do this. Sometimes (especially in the towns) they were permitted to bring German law with them. The amount of cultural interchange was very considerable and, of course, of great mutual benefit. But the Germans and the Slavs did not tend to merge together into one people in this third zone of medieval German expansion eastwards, either completely (as in

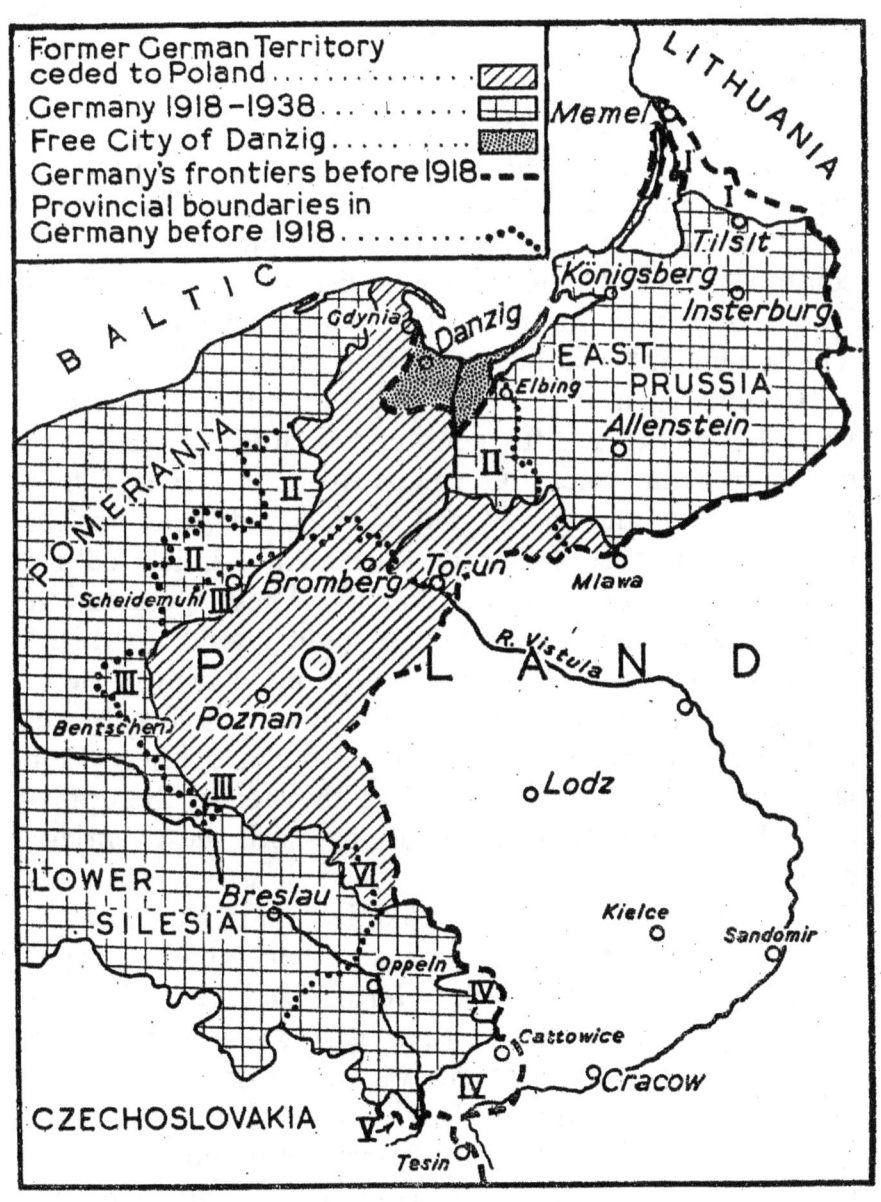

MAP 6. THE POLISH CORRIDOR, 1919–39
(*Compare with the maps on pp. 16 and 26*)

the trans-Elbe lands) or even partially (as in Pomerania and Silesia). The Germans remained an immigrant community, referred to as 'Germans' by the Slavs around them, even when subjects of the kings of Poland or of Bohemia. Nor were they regarded as in any way a menace to the political integrity of these kingdoms, even where the latter were at war with the Empire or the states of Germany. The technique of the 'fifth column' had not yet been born to disturb the Germans in Polish Silesia or in the Tatra mountains of Slovakia. The same can be said of those who settled farther afield in Siebenburgen, in the Hungarian province of Transylvania, from the twelfth century onwards. There were probably some 70,000 Germans living in Transylvania by A.D. 1500, and the legend of the Pied Piper makes reference to these far-away settlements, inhabited by Browning's 'tribe in Transylvania'. These Germans in Transylvania became Hungarian (and later Rumanian) citizens in the way Germans emigrating to Pennsylvania in the eighteenth century became first British subjects and later American citizens. They did not desert their language or their culture, but they transferred their political allegiance without reservation—until the twentieth century.

A fourth zone of German colonization in Europe was, as has been seen already, of a rather different type. Although they thoroughly Germanized East Prussia (lying beyond the lower Vistula) by rigorous colonization and by exterminating the native Slavs who resisted, the Teutonic Knights and the Knights of the Sword, pursuing their 'crusade' along the Baltic shore, set up no more than a skeleton-occupation of Lithuania, Latvia and Esthonia. Here the Germans as feudal overlords ruled over a Slav-populated countryside, but only really congregated in any

GERMAN EXPANSION IN EUROPE

numbers in the score or so of towns they had founded. These towns remained members of the Hanseatic league even after the power of the Teutonic Knights was broken in the fifteenth century and the knights were forced to do homage to the Polish king for the lands they continued to occupy. From Poland the Baltic provinces were eventually to pass to Russia, and in our own century to pass back and forth between the two again—with a brief interlude of independence from 1919 to 1939 and an even briefer period of re-integration with the German Empire (the 'Great' German Reich of Adolf Hitler) from 1941 to 1944. In both of these interludes, as indeed in the whole of the history of the Baltic provinces since the days of the Teutonic Knights, the former Hanseatic towns and the German 'Balt' population (although only

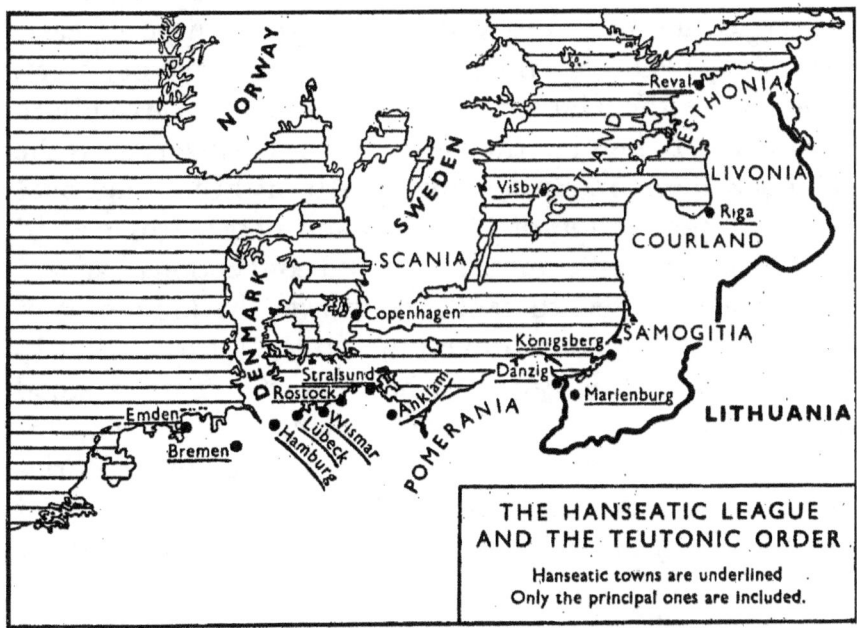

MAP 7—*after Shorter Cambridge Medieval History*

small islands in a Slav and Finno-Ugrian[1] sea) have played a very important, at times a dominating, part in the life of the area. The strange case of Alfred Rosenberg (born in Esthonia in 1893 and executed at Nürnberg as a war criminal in 1946) has already been mentioned.

Thus there was a check to German expansion eastwards in the fourteenth and fifteenth centuries, which lasted for over three hundred years, like the check to westward expansion that occurred when Louis XI of France seized the greater part of Burgundy and his successors went after the natural frontier of the Rhine. But this expansion, while it lasted, had been a very remarkable one. By the year 1340 the Holy Roman Empire probably contained about 12,000,000 inhabitants.

New German dynasties, coming to the fore only in the later Middle Ages, managed to attach those remnants which could be saved out of this great surge of eastward expansion, to their other territories farther west. Such were the Habsburgs in Austria, the Luxemburg family in Bohemia, the Wettins in Meissen and the Hohenzollerns in Brandenburg. All of these ruled over a mixed population of Germans and non-Germans and had many foreign commitments and connections. When, from the seventeenth century onwards, the kingdoms of Poland and Bohemia broke up, and the Ottoman Turks evacuated central Europe, these 'new' dynasties stood ready to expand at the latter's expense and to weld together the scattered fragments of their existing territories with these new acquisitions. Though the Electors of Brandenburg proved to be the most successful of all these new dynasts in their acquisitions, several of the others did very well also, and the lands they secured in the east

---

[1] The bulk of the inhabitants of Esthonia are not Slavs but are ethnically related to the Finns and the Magyars.

were very often (as when Brandenburg obtained the Duchy of Prussia[1]) larger than their existing dominions. Nevertheless, even when the kingdoms of Bohemia and of Poland had been extinguished, the high-water mark of German expansion eastwards in the Middle Ages was not again reached. It remained the ambition of nineteenth- and twentieth-century Germans, their national feeling sharpened by the era of Liberation and by unification under Prussia, to secure every one of these territories once again. These long-lost outposts were made the basis for modern claims (such as that for the Memel territory) which have played a catastrophic role in twentieth-century history. The Germans of the National Socialist Third Reich of Adolf Hitler finally made a bid to re-incorporate all the lands in Europe that Germans had ever colonized since the days of Henry the Fowler. They very nearly succeeded.

[1] That is to say *East* Prussia as we know it.

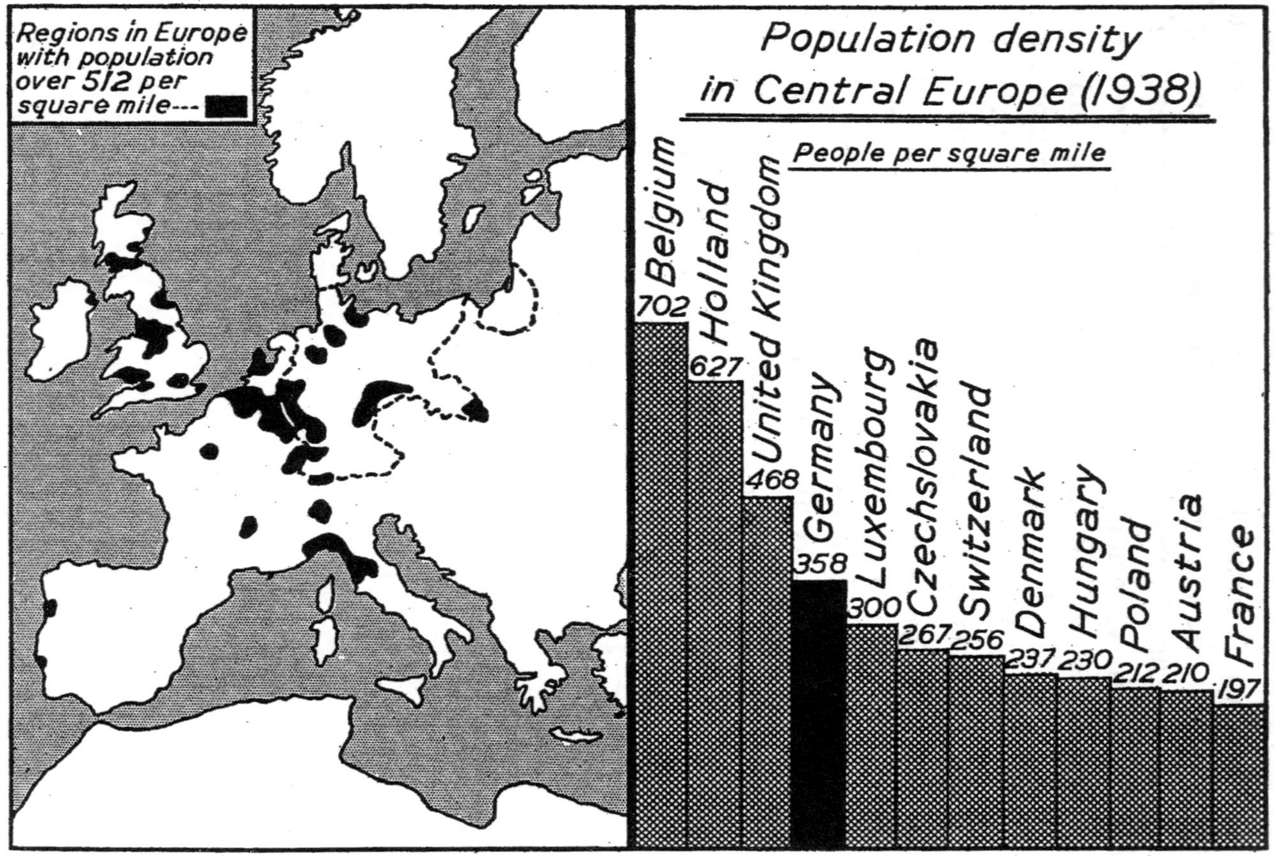

MAP 8

Population density in Central Europe (1938)

People per square mile

Country	People per square mile
Belgium	702
Holland	627
United Kingdom	468
Germany	358
Luxembourg	300
Czechoslovakia	267
Switzerland	256
Denmark	237
Hungary	230
Poland	212
Austria	210
France	197

Regions in Europe with population over 512 per square mile — ■

Part II   *The Resources of Germany*

CHAPTER I

FOREST AND CLEARING

THE land of Germany was once more than three-quarters covered by forests. Since Neolithic times these forests have gradually been reduced until they occupy just over a quarter of the area of the country. Even that is a higher proportion than in any other country of central or western Europe. The forest industries therefore have remained of great importance in the lives of the Germans, and the forest has always played a great part in German literature and legend, from the medieval *Niebelungenlied* (and the older sagas on which it was partially based) to Wagner's nineteenth-century re-fashioning of it to provide the setting of his great music-drama cycle *The Ring*. Forest murmurs indeed have always echoed in the ears of the people of Germany, and the primeval forest, the *Urwald* as it is so expressively named, can still strike awe in the mind of a German. Anyone who has stood in the outer rampart of that somewhat flamboyant modern reconstruction of a Roman fort on the *limes* above Frankfurt-am-Main, known as the Saalburg, and has gazed over the unbroken forested slopes of the Taunus, stretching to the horizon, can recapture that feeling of awe of the early Germans for the great forests that surrounded and hemmed in their meagre settlements.

    The men of the old Stone Age, and the near-men who preceded them, lacked the tools or the skill to clear Germany's forests and probably clung to the unforested plains and uplands and the riverside meadows and cave-pocked bluffs, but Neolithic man seems to have been able to burn or fell trees in the less dense forests and parkland, especially of the great loess belt that stretches across Germany from the Rhine to Silesia. While forest-free land was naturally favoured by Neolithic and early Bronze Age man in Germany, just as Salisbury Plain for similar reasons became a favourite centre of Neolithic and Bronze Age culture in England, archaeologists and geographers are now inclined to think that much of the north German heathland that the Germanic tribes poured into around 500 B.C. had once been forested. But of course the amount of forest clearance was as yet pitifully small, and it is estimated that even a full millenium later about A.D. 500, the area of Germany was still at least 70 per cent forested.

The Germanic tribes indeed settled in a series of forest-free or cleared areas divided from each other by deep and impenetrable forests, such as the *Frankenwald*, the *Thuringerwald* and the *Bayrischerwald*, the very names of which indicate the tribes they bounded. Their communications and trade with each other, and their warlike expeditions against each other, had to be conducted, not across these great forests, but by ancient treeless ridge routes or through the river valleys which ribboned through the forests, along alluvial plains or deep defiles. The East Franks, from their strong point of *Frankfurt*, thus expanded eastwards up the Main valley into Thuringia until they came up against the great forested highlands in which the Main rises. There were other great forests between them and the Bavarians. Between the Bavarians and the Swabians stretched the great *Black Forest* which has continued to bear that name to this day.[1]

[1] See map on p. 8.

Although there was some early settlement in the Frisian islands and on the north German plain once covered by the glaciers of the Ice Age, the soil there was not very fertile and in coastal areas was liable to flooding, so the bulk of the Germanic population was to be found on the more fertile soil south of a line running approximately from the site of Cologne to that of Magdeburg. Here in the loess and limestone belt which stretches across Germany below that line, in river valleys such as the Rhine, the Moselle, the Neckar and the Main, and on highlands under 2,000 feet such as the Bavarian plateau, the Germanic tribes settled down to an agricultural economy. They reclaimed waste-land and drained swamps, and increased the size of their forest clearings, but only piecemeal and on a small scale until the great movement of the *Völkerwanderung* was over and the tribes began to look upon the land they were occupying as their permanent homes. Then, from about A.D. 800, came an era of systematic and large-scale forest-clearing and land-reclamation that lasted for over five hundred years. By about the year A.D. 1350 much of the accessible land under 2,000 feet (up to which level above the sea rye could by grown over most of Germany) had been cleared, and some of Germany's smaller and more isolated forests had disappeared completely. The 'Era of the Clearance of Forests' (or *Rodungszeit*) may have left much of the ancient Hercynian forest of south-central Germany undented, but it nevertheless changed the face of much of the country. A network of trade routes was opened up through and across the forests, and towns and cities began to spring up (they were little more than villages in most cases) along these routes, sometimes in what had once been the depths of the primeval forest.

After A.D. 1350 population pressure eased[1] and the great forest-clearing age was over. A country formerly nearly three-quarters forested was very much less than half covered with forests. Forest clearance has never been on the same scale since, and the last hundred years has seen a policy of re-afforestation initiated.

By the twentieth century a full three-quartars of the area of Germany was farmland (the forests occupied 27 per cent of the country's area in 1939) and produced fully four-fifths of the food consumed by the German people. Most of the farms (and especially in the west and south-west) were on a very small scale, and nine-tenths of the farmers owned their farms. The whole economy of the country had been changed by forest clearance, which had been necessary before it could become a populous, highly industrialized and extensively urbanized nation (three-quarters of its population lived in towns by 1939). The foundations of the great material advances of the last hundred years were thus laid in the Era of the Clearing of Forests.

[1] See p. 81.

CHAPTER II

RIVER AND FORTRESS

THE Empire of Charles the Great was almost completely rural and agricultural. The sites he chose for his palaces and strong-points may have been those of former Roman settlements—such as Aachen (Aix-la-Chapelle)—but he did not rebuild or re-people them on an urban scale. Aachen in his day had a very tiny built-up area and the cathedral was the first substantial stone building to be put up north of the Alps since the decay of Roman power. Some of his other palaces—such as that at Wimpfen on the banks of the Neckar river (in Württemberg)—were located on sites which never did develop into towns. The urban settlement was indeed not part of the Carolingian scheme of things, and the primitive subsistence economy of the time would not have provided for any large agglomerations of population within the walls of one place.

At the crossing points of routes, at the confluences of rivers or alongside monasteries, or bishops' or princes' palaces, there was a small amount of trading (usually quite intermittent), mostly carried on by itinerant merchants who (like the strolling players of a later date out of which the dignified theatrical profession of Knights and Dames and Chevaliers of our own day has developed) were regarded as little better than rogues and vagabonds —men without land and without law. It was in fact their freedom from the jurisdiction of any local lord that was to give these strolling merchants their strength when they did start living together in towns (as Henri Pirenne has pointed out in his brilliant study of the rise of *Medieval Cities*[1]), but that was not to be yet.

The humble beginnings of the revival of town life in Germany and in the rest of western Europe north of the Alps (in Italy there was no complete break in the urban tradition, though many towns were abandoned and the others dwindled to shadows of their former selves) came in the shape of *urbes mercatorum* already referred to, in the eighth and ninth centuries. These sometimes transient 'merchant towns' were all that the Carolingian Empire knew of urban development. We would not have recognized them as towns or even as large villages.

It was natural that the first real towns of the Holy Roman Empire should develop on the sites of old German and Frankish strong-points, where stockades and other means of defence against marauding raiders already existed. Some of these had previously been Roman settlements but others had not. Of the fifteen such towns that appear to have existed by the end of the tenth century about nine were on Roman sites—the most easterly of these being Regensberg on the Danube. The remaining six—Courtrai and Dortmund in the north-west, Goslar (the favourite residence of Otto the Great), Würzburg and Bamberg in the central part of the Empire and Magdeburg on the Elbe in the east—had not existed before Carolingian times.

In the eleventh and twelfth centuries upwards of three hundred more towns came into existence in Germany but by the end of the fourteenth there were fully 2,000, so it is the four hundred years between A.D. 1000 and 1400 that was the great age of the foundation and building of towns in the German Middle Ages. Indeed,

[1] Title of the English translation (1924).

most German towns of any consequence existing in our own day west of the Elbe were founded before 1400.

The twelfth century was the great period of the consolidation of urban rights and privileges in Germany, communal rights being first obtained by the citizens of Cologne (in A.D. 1106) and of Goslar (in 1107). These had to be secured from the local magnates who owned the land on which the towns were situated (the 'free imperial city' was to be a later manifestation) and, to begin with, these were usually bishops or abbots rather than secular lords. The building of a cathedral and of a bishop's palace had inevitably attracted a small informal urban nucleus, where the bishop's officials, servants, craftsmen and workmen lived and enjoyed his protection. It was only logical that this *Domfreiheit* should be extended to the merchants and traders who settled down alongside and around the 'cathedral close' or the monastery gate. The fortified manor-houses of the secular magnates contained their handful of retainers, but did not serve so well as ready-made nuclei for the development of towns. The feudal castle did not play the significant role in the development of town life in medieval Germany that it did in England or France or even Spain, for while the imperial authority remained strong (until the late twelfth century, intermittently) the building of castles by the local nobility remained under the ban of the Empire. Barely twenty German towns founded before the year A.D. 1200 can trace their origin to a castle-nucleus, although many were to grow up in that way during the feudal anarchy of the thirteenth and fourteenth centuries.

While a number of the earliest towns of medieval Germany did not grow up on important trade routes (Aachen again is a good example), the majority of them will be found on one or other of the east-west roads that the merchants and traders followed. As the most important of these was the one going from the Netherlands through Cologne and eastwards to Magdeburg just to the north of the line dividing the lowlands from the uplands of Germany (the 600-foot contour),[1] a majority of the early towns were to be found in north Germany (a proportion of about three to two), and this perhaps explains why the great Hanseatic League of the cities of the north which reached its heyday in the fourteenth century was always so much more important than the Swabian League of south German cities which flourished at about the same time. The south German cities tended, much more than those of the north, to be strung along the river system (on the middle Rhine almost like beads), for the highlands which divided these valleys were still sparsely inhabited and many of their forests uncleared. On the other hand, the north German plain, where it widened out eastwards past the Weser to the Elbe and beyond, was also (north of the great trade route already mentioned) sparsely populated and not very suitable for urban growth.

Traffic between north and south, on a scale comparable to that between east and west, did not develop before the thirteenth century (by which time the great era of the clearing of forests was almost over), but, when it did, it provided a stimulus to the founding of many new towns on hitherto remote and unpromising sites, especially in Bavaria and Tyrol, across which the traders took their goods on the way to and from Italy and the Levant, and across which the Crusaders had sometimes made their pilgrimage without benefit of much in the way of urban amenities.

[1] See map facing p. 1.

Another great stimulus to later medieval urban development was of course the eastward advance (even though much of it was politically transient) of German settlement and civilization. There were few towns in the eastland (beyond the Elbe) before systematic German colonization began there, but between A.D. 1200 and 1400 over fifteen hundred towns were established there, many of them on a 'planned basis', not only as regards their street system and the location of their public buildings, but also as regards their distance from each other (eight hours travel apart was the spacing-out that was regarded as ideal). These new eastern towns were indeed almost mass-produced, adopting, for instance, the street-plan of Lübeck (founded in 1158), or the law of Magdeburg or of other 'mother cities' farther west. Most of these were in no sense 'satellite towns', but completely independent developments which had nevertheless gone to the best models and made use of the ripe experience of earlier foundations, just as did the towns of the North American continent (even to the extent of borrowing the names of the 'mother' settlements in Europe, which the east German town did not) some three or four hundred years later.

Here is not the place to tell the detailed story of the rich town life of Germany during the later Middle Ages, which bequeathed so much wealth and so many architectural and artistic glories to the modern age, but it must be remembered that, although the towns were never again to be completely blotted out of existence (even by the depredations of the Black Death or of the Thirty Years War), they ceased to expand and also lost most of their independence and privileges in and after the fifteenth century. By the end of the Middle Ages (A.D. 1500) there were perhaps three thousand towns in the

Holy Roman Empire—by contrast with the fifteen in the year 1000—many of them very small by our standards, but several of them very large. While over five-sixths of the towns contained less than five hundred inhabitants each, Cologne and Lübeck each had over 30,000 and a dozen others had over 10,000. Urban population had increased very rapidly in Germany up to about A.D. 1350, and then went on increasing more gradually until by the year 1500 upwards of 15 per cent of Germany's population lived in towns. The increase went on at a slackened pace until the early seventeenth century (on the eve of the Thirty Years War), when Germany's urban population reached its highest level within the boundaries of the old city walls—and there was little of a permanent nature outside them, for obvious reasons in such troubled days—after which there came two full centuries of stagnation (from mid-seventeenth to mid-nineteenth century). Subsequently, the Industrial Revolution was once again to stimulate German urban growth on a scale comparable to (though very different in many ways from) the developments of the twelfth, thirteenth and early fourteenth centuries.

By the nineteenth century, the cities of Germany had long since ceased to need the protection of their medieval walls (which even in the seventeenth had stood them of little avail against the formidable siege artillery of the day), but it was not until after the foundation of the Bismarckian 'Second Empire' that they began to throw down these walls and expand their administrative areas into the 'suburban' regions that were beginning to grow up outside them. The new expansion, when it came, was to be very rapid, but while Germany saw her greatest rate of population growth in all her history between the years 1870 and 1914, very few entirely *new* towns were founded during those years. The main expansion was in the size of towns already founded before the end of the Middle Ages. Even between A.D. 1500 and 1850 very few new towns had been created, the most notable of course being the city of Berlin, destined to be the capital of Brandenburg-Prussia and then of a united Germany. A few new ports came into existence (and even more decayed) with the shift in the emphasis of trade from the narrow seas to the world oceans, and a few *Residenz-Städte*, or provincial capitals, sprang up in new places in the seventeenth and eighteenth centuries, when every petty German prince wanted to build his own Versailles. But that was all.

Germany's urban greatness still rests securely upon its medieval foundations. When the city of Cologne was virtually obliterated by the great air raids of 1942-4 it was the medieval city, within the former walls and the great ring of boulevards marking their limits, with its romanesque churches and its Hanseatic halls and merchant houses that disappeared for ever—not the modern Cologne beyond those walls, which suffered less and is rapidly being rebuilt. Cologne within the ancient walls will also no doubt be rebuilt, but it will not be old Cologne. Nevertheless, the *Domplatz* will remain for everybody the centre of the city.

CHAPTER III

THE PEASANTS AND THE LAND

'WE know little of Germanic society before the great invasions' is the verdict of a great authority, Marc Bloch, and indeed we have had to unlearn recently a great deal of what we once thought we knew. Once upon a time Tacitus, the renowned Roman author of *Germania* and the *Annals*, written during the first century A.D., was our chief guide to the life that the Germanic tribes lived immediately before and during their attacks on the frontiers of the Roman Empire. Now we have to realize that, while much of the information that Tacitus gave is still valuable, it cannot be safely used without confirmation by non-literary sources, and that he was as much a moralist as a geographer or an historian, seeking to contrast the supposed free, democratic, rural, uninhibited existence of the Germans with the decadence, and the political and other repressions, of Imperial Rome. It was the old game (for Greek writers had played it before him) of extolling the 'noble savage' by imagining in him all the virtues civilized man seemed to have lost, and it was still being played by Rousseau and others seventeen hundred years after Tacitus. In reality, the primitive Germans were neither so moral nor so democratic as Tacitus chose to imagine. They had fewer virtues, and also rather more vices than the sloth and excessive addiction to strong liquor and gambling that Tacitus mentions. Archaeological and other evidence has considerably modified his picture.

While the Germans of the *Völkerwanderung* had, by and large, become agriculturalists, their rural economy was a simple one, being based mainly upon grain-crops, and they continued to keep considerable herds of cattle and swine. They did not feel tied to the soil in any intimate way and often exhausted the land they were tilling in several years, and then moved on, like the early American farmers were to do. Where they did settle more or less permanently, they practised a simple two-crop or two-field system, leaving the land fallow every other year. This two-field system persisted indeed in many parts of Germany into the later Middle Ages, when it was in process of being supplanted by the more efficient three-field system.

In very few places was land (other than waste-land) held in common or divided more or less equally. Even in Friesland, where equal division took place among the settlers, there was nothing like the annual re-allocation of land which Tacitus described. Almost everywhere among the German tribes there were deep class distinctions. Some families possessed large tracts of land, and others very little; some were landless and many were in a servile state. The primitive Germans also kept slaves, though not on the scale that the Romans did. The warrior class did not demean itself, in most tribes, by tilling the soil, and the peasant who did so had a lower social status. The chief and kings were not elected, but were those who were best able to seize and to retain power by force or guile. A species of low cunning was as highly regarded as any of the manly virtues, and the primitive German heroes celebrated in the sagas and the *Niebelungenlied* and afterwards given a new lease of literary life by Richard Wagner, all pitted their wits against one another even more often than they drew their swords on each other. Siegmund, a guileless sort of hero, only lasted for one act of the *Ring*. Alberich, the cunning dwarf, is on and off the stage almost throughout the whole cycle.

Tacitus seems to have been correct in characterizing the Germans with a dislike of urban settlements and with a preference for living 'scattered and apart' from each other in their primitive state, for even when they crossed the Rhine, and, as did the Franks, occupied Roman provinces that had supported a vigorous town life, they made little use of the Roman cities or their ruins until after the Carolingian period, as has been seen. One of the oddest sights of the early medieval landscape of Western Europe must have been an arch or a basilica, a stone *castella* or a great wall, standing up in the midst of a deserted and weed-grown site, with, a short distance away, the Germanic invaders living in hovels of wattle and mud, or, at most, primitive wooden huts, surrounded by their fields of corn, and their cattle pasturing in the waste-land they did not cultivate. What did these invaders make of the *Porta Nigra* at Trier, or of the amphitheatre at Arles—within which, centuries later, a whole medieval settlement (when urban life began again) was to find room and to spare?

The typical Germanic village of what have been called (by Koebner) 'Tacitean' days, thus seems to have consisted of scattered homesteads, growing corn in long strips rather than large fields and pasturing the animals on any waste or woodland beyond the strips. If there was forest on the edge of the settlement the inhabitants did not clear it, though the cattle might stray into it and the more hardy of them (for they held it in superstitious awe) might go hunting in it. The waste-land was of tremendous importance to these primitive rural settlements, and often large tracts of it, uncultivated, but by no means untillable (though it might need clearing, draining, or levelling), separated the different communities. The land-hunger of the central and later Middle Ages, which was to drive both the peasants and their lords to covet this waste-land, had not yet occurred, for population-pressure was as yet slight.

As the Germanic tribes settled down into their permanent territories when the age of wandering ended at about the beginning of the Carolingian period, their use of the land and the structure of their society (about which we know much more than in the period of Tacitus, especially from the study of the codes of laws—such as those of the Burgundians in France and of the Saxons in Germany and of Ine of Wessex (A.D. 700) in England—which they drew up about this time) began to assume local variations. The equal division of the soil by the Friesians has already been mentioned: Thuringia (which came under Saxon control just after A.D. 700) seems to have had strong class distinctions and (as it was a heavily forested area) a number of the new-type forest-villages (*Waldhufendörfer*) with the houses built in a double row along an axis or 'main street', their land streaming out from each in a long thin ribbon through the cleared area up into the woods, as well as the more familiar nucleated villages (*Haufendörfer*) of scattered homesteads in the unforested areas. Here, as in Lower Saxony proper, there seems to have been three clearly defined social classes, the nobility (*Edelinger*), the freemen (*Frilinger*), and the servile, or bound-to-the-soil (*Laten*). There were few or no slaves, for the slave-culture that Merovingian times inherited (to a reduced extent) from the Roman Empire, had practically disappeared by the Carolingian era. Those who remained were domestic slaves, usually captured in the wars against the Slavonic tribes to the East, or even bought from them. The very name 'slave' originated in this way, and did not evolve out of the the Latin *servus*, as might have been imagined.

Thus, after the *Völkerwanderung* was over, the German tribes settled down to till the soil with two classes of peasants, the free and unfree, each class with its own piece of land, but the latter giving labour and other service to a local magnate for it. The freeman would either own his land absolutely or pay rent for it. Gradually, during the troubled times of the Dark Ages, these two classes of peasant became 'pressed together' (Koebner) more and more closely, the free cultivator binding himself in service to a lord in order to secure protection, and by the end of the tenth century the old type of *Frilinger* was already rare. This was the low ebb in the fortunes of the Germanic peasantry from which it was to rise through the eleventh, twelfth and thirteenth centuries to a much more favourable position.

The Alemanni, the Bavarians and the east Franks (or Franconians) followed the same general pattern as the Thuringians and the Saxons in their rural and class development, although the west Franks (in what was to become France) came much more under the influence of the remnants of the Roman tradition. Though slavery died out among them also, their villages were recognizable descendants of the Roman *villa* system and each tended to have a planned nucleus surrounding a lord's dwelling or an open space. Class distinctions were equally strong here in the *seigneurie* type of domain that came in with the early development (long before the same stage was reached in Germany) of feudal tenures and practices in France.

The golden age of the medieval German peasant came between the eleventh century and the Black Death in the middle of the fourteenth. The spread of leasehold tenure (especially in Lower Saxony, Westphalia, North Hessen, Bavaria and the Swabian uplands) allowed him greater freedom in the disposal of land and freed him from many customary dues. In the eleventh century there had been a few small free proprietors in Friesland, Saxony and Thuringia, but the vast majority were dependent. By the end of the thirteenth century a much wider degree of personal freedom had been attained. Servile tenants tended to have become peasant proprietors; seigneurial burdens were becoming steadily lighter; tenants were benefiting from the rise in value of agricultural produce and from the demand for it in the new and enlarged towns, and this also gave them some liquid capital. Also, if they were not satisfied with their lot they could migrate to the towns, to which there was a continuous drain of the most able and enterprising peasants. At the same time the prosperity of the feudal lords decreased, especially where they had commuted services for money, which was now worth less than it had been when this was done. Many lords mortgaged their lands and were subjected to foreclosure. The peasants found themselves best situated in central Germany (where seigneurial institutions had never obtained so firm a hold), but less fortunately placed in the north-west (Lower Saxony and Westphalia) on the one hand, and in the south-west (in Baden, in Württemberg and what is now German Switzerland) on the other. In south-west Germany, in particular, the land was divided up by inheritance into smaller and smaller holdings, and after the great safety-valve of eastern colonization was closed after the end of the thirteenth century, and the great age of forest clearance ceased at about the same time, the situation was ripe there for the rural discontents of the fifteenth century and the peasant risings of the sixteenth. The new towns and the sovereign princes who had taken over control of the land from its former feudal lords, in many cases proved as harsh in demanding services and rents from the peasants as their former masters, yet the tradition of unquestioning obedience had been broken, In addition, the labour shortage following the Black Death[1] put many peasants in a much more independent position, though it also created a 'landless class'.

Thus, from the fourteenth century onwards, the German peasant lost his former security and was subjected to all the strains and stresses of man in a society once more in a state of flux. Improved agricultural methods (including the wide adoption of the three-field system) did not provide complete compensation for his lost security. Unlike the peasant class in England (but like the French), the German peasant did not find himself—except in a few areas—a completely free man by the end of the fifteenth century. Even as late as the eighteenth century (although he had not been subjected to the depredations of successive enclosure movements) he still continued to bear many burdens inherited from the Middle Ages. The west German 'free tenant' continued to pay his *Zins* to his lord; the central German peasant still did labour service (even if the 'boon work' was slight to the point of being ludicrous in places), while the unfortunate peasant in east Germany had slipped back to the status of a complete serf, on great

---

[1] See further p. 81.

estates operated virtually as *latifundia*. The benevolent despots of the eighteenth century did something to remedy this situation (especially on reclaimed land and in regions evacuated by the Ottoman Turks) but it was not until the era of the French Revolutionary and Napoleonic invasions of Germany (1793-1814) that serfdom received its death blow there. Stein's edict of Emancipation in Prussia (1807) abolished serfdom in that state, and Hardenburg's decree of 1811 provided for the purchase on easy terms of hereditary tenures by their peasant-holders. But the amount of land these peasants had to give up to extinguish their burdens (from one-third to a half of their holdings, if they could not find a sum equal to 25 years' rent) reduced these in many cases to an uneconomic size. In the eighteen-thirties, forties, fifties and sixties, many preferred to sell up and emigrate to America, where land could be had for nothing, or next to nothing. Serfdom also disappeared in the Habsburg lands after 1848, but the obligation to pay rent remained, and this was often too great a burden, after years of economic depression. The middle years of the nineteenth century were thus yet another period of hard times for the German peasant.

Only after the unification of 1871 did Germany really become a country of free landowning peasants—except in the eastern areas where the large *Junker* estates remained. By the year 1907, 93 per cent of Germany's farmers owned the land they tilled and 82 per cent of the farm areas of the country was cultivator-occupied. Old-fashioned methods continued to be used on many of these small farms (a majority were under 12 acres in extent), and the medieval open-field system persisted in many places, with its uneconomical strip cultivation. Only after 1918 did the rulers of the Weimar Republic set about a compensated re-arrangement of land-ownership in a systematic way, and by 1929 had re-arranged 8 million acres—leaving another 6 million in their former unsatisfactory state. Even the Weimar republic failed to solve the problem for the Junker estates in the east, and this was indeed one of the difficulties that played into the hands of Hitler, who also in his turn failed to modernize or democratize the land system east of the Elbe, This was, of course, done ruthlessly and effectively after 1945, but by that time the Junkers had all disappeared and so had most of the German farmers, and much of the land in question had passed out of German into Polish or Russian hands.

The peasants of west Germany in the years after 1945 had to find space in their villages (there was no room for them in the war-devastated towns) for millions of refugees from the east, and a new land-hunger comparable to that of the late Middle Ages and the middle nineteenth century, began to develop there. This has yet to be assuaged.

CHAPTER IV

THE NOBILITY
AND THEIR PRIVILEGES

THE drinking, roistering, gambling 'free German' of the pages of Tacitus is really the fighting man of the Germanic tribes. Tacitus generalized from him and had little to say about the working or servile peasant. As elsewhere, the warrior considered manual labour to be beneath him. His women ran the household, and his servants, bondsmen or slaves did the domestic and field work. If he were a leader, a chief or a king, he owned wide lands, but others tilled them for him, in so far as they were cultivated at all.

The *Völkerwanderung* tended to prolong the privileged status of this 'happy warrior', for his tribe was in constant need to be fighting someone or other to maintain or to extend its new-won lands. Usually he secured landed property himself when the tribe finally settled down, but some warriors remained the personal retainers of the chiefs, living with and maintained by them as bodyguards or garrison. Yet, gradually, the warrior class (with the exception of these last) had to turn its attention more and more to the running of estates and domains. The *latifundia* or *villa* culture of the Romano-Gallic areas did not develop in Germany, certainly not east of the Rhine, as has been seen, but the 'lord' assumed seigneurial privileges similar to those of his counterpart in Gaul.

Feudalism came late into Germany. It was imported from France and it was never so completely adopted there as in France. In the north, in particular, the old tribal or 'class' organization persisted, and fief-holding and the oath of fealty were only partially introduced. A tidy network of governmental feudalism such as William the Conqueror imposed upon England, never existed in Germany. Allodial tenure (not involving any service to a lord) was, by contrast with England, widespread in Germany—especially in areas where the forests had to be cleared and the no-man's-land to the east settled—and indeed, the farther one went from the western and Gallic 'cradle of feudalism' (the region between the Rhine and the Loire), the less comprehensively was feudalism 'received' in the lands of Germany.

The great warrior families among the invading tribes had laid their hands on very extensive patrimonies. The Frankish leaders took over and started up again the estates which the Romano-Gallic nobility had occupied before them west of the Rhine, and the chiefs of the Allemanni laid claim to equally large though less 'improved' tracts farther east. 'Family forests' were not unusual in the Rhineland, but, as has been seen, it was not until centuries later that these began to be cleared and turned over to agricultural uses. The Saxon *Edelinger* (nobility) came into the possession of equally wide tracts, and then extended these when Thuringia was conquered and colonization beyond the Elbe was commenced. In Lower Saxony the *Frilinger* class stood between the nobility and the servile tenants, and elsewhere the tenants in Sergeantry (*Dienstlehen*) with their labour-fiefs—although they had to engage directly in the tilling of the land—themselves evolved into a sort of inferior knightly class. The more enterprising and fortunate of these, holding their land directly from the Emperor, or getting into that happy position by the extinction of intermediate authorities, might join the class of Imperial Knights, as proud as, but much poorer than, the great landed nobility. These would later on have to engage in trade, extort dues and fines from merchants and travellers, or hire themselves out as mercenaries, to make ends meet, while there was, for two centuries or more, the great escapist outlet for them of combining virtue with necessity and going on a crusade.

By the twelfth century a fully-fledged noble class had emerged in Germany, not very dissimilar from that which existed in England and France and sharing all the traditions and practices of western chivalry. An English or a French knight would feel at home in a German castle or court and a German knight would know what to do in an English or French one. The great difference lay in the lowered prestige of the monarchy in Germany and its reduced authority over the nobility and the knightly class. In the twelfth and thirteenth centuries the authority declined disastrously and the efforts of the Hohenstauffen emperors to use the institutions of governmental feudalism to bolster it up failed. The great noblemen, and especially the Electors of the Empire were gradually relieved by the Emperor of all but nominal feudal services, especially where (as in Austria) they were engaged in the extensive settlement and colonization of March or frontier lands. When the great magnates rebelled (like Henry the Lion of Saxony), it was impossible to crush them completely even after defeat in battle, so strong was their local backing. Concession after concession (and particularly Frederick II's statute of A.D. 1132) further undermined imperial authority and the disastrous Interregnum of the thirteenth century virtually destroyed it. The Golden Bull of A.D. 1356 indicates how completely the princes and magnates had won their independence of the Emperor a century later. The reception of Roman Civil Law in Germany (A.D. 1495) gave legal re-inforcement to their position, and the opportunities provided by the Reformation removed all further barriers to their complete *de facto* sovereignty.

As the Electors and greater territorial magnates went up in the world to become sovereign princes, the lesser nobility and the knights fell behind in the race. Some lost their lands by foreclosure during the economic blizzards of the fourteenth and fifteenth centuries; others, losing their servile workers by manumission, by the Black Death or by migration to the new towns, could no longer work their estates and sold up in despair, sometimes themselves going to live in towns and engaging in trade. Those traditionalists and die-hards who managed to hang on to dwindling estates and revenues (in terms of purchasing power) into the sixteenth century, became a sort of 'depressed upper class', too shabby as it were to appear at court and yet too proud to do an honest day's work. Goetz von Berlichingen, later immortalized and somewhat over-romanticized by Goethe, was such a type, and he ended his days in a futile and belated attempt to make common cause with the disgruntled peasants of the rising of A.D. 1525, though he had really little in common with them except a strong objection to things as they were.

Nothing has been said about the ecclesiastical electors and notables who held so much land in Germany during the Middle Ages, because their privileges and their fortunes ran so parallel to those of their secular counterparts. It is true that their loyalties were torn by the

Investiture controversy and other phases of the struggle between Pope and Emperor more fiercely than those of the secular nobility, but this did not necessarily affect very materially the way in which they ruled over their estates and their peasants and serfs. Many of them, such as the Archbishop-Electors of Cologne, were among the most powerful and splendid of the princes of Germany during the Middle Ages, and they exploited their secular privileges to the full. Those of them who survived the Reformation continued to enjoy their lands, and all that these brought them, until the end of the eighteenth or the beginning of the nineteenth century. They were on the whole no better and no worse as rulers or as landlords than the secular nobility. As subjects of the Empire, they were, if anything, even more intractable, for there was always that other allegiance, to Rome, for them to consider—and exploit.

A remarkable extension of the activities of the German knightly class of the Middle Ages was provided by the colonization of the north-east. Here the Teutonic Knights and the Knights of the Sword, with their monkish asceticism and discipline, but their thoroughly secular ruthlessness in battle, in trade and in diplomacy, became a new ruling class both in the towns and in the countryside, surrounded by free German peasant-immigrants and merchants, and exploiting a Slavonic serf-population. They did much better for themselves in this new empire, while it lasted, than did their fellows who stayed at home—most of them came from the knightly class and lesser nobility of south and west Germany—and the Baltic lands conveniently provided, for two further centuries, the same sort of safety-valve to roving ambitions that the Crusades had supplied up to the beginning of the thirteenth. It must be remembered, too, that not only knights from other parts of Germany, but from all over western Europe, flocked to the Baltic lands, as mercenaries or as settlers. Even the 'parfit gentil knight' of Geoffrey Chaucer had been there in his day:

> Ful ofte tyme he hadde the bord bigonne
> Aboven alle naciouns in Pruce.
> In Lettow hadde he reysed and in Ruce,
> No cristen man so ofte of his degree.

The Teutonic Knights may not all have been the double-dyed villains they are shown as in the Soviet film *Alexander Nevski*, but altruism was not their long suit. With their defeat by the Poles at Tannenberg in 1410 the Teutonic Knights lost much of their prestige and had to retreat westwards or break their political connection with Germany, but many of them continued to live on, as a privileged class, in the Baltic lands, after the dissolution of the Order. Their descendants became the 'Baltic Barons' of modern times. Now they too are no more. Even their age-old resourcefulness and adroitness did not suffice to let them turn themselves into Commissars!

NOTE: The fortunes of the nobility and the knightly class of Germany have here been followed up to the beginning of modern times, when the maturing of the sovereign territorial state placed them in a new situation. From then on it is difficult to speak of them collectively, and they developed in different ways in Austria, in Brandenburg-Prussia and in the many lesser states of Germany. By the nineteenth century they could no longer be said to belong together any more—not, at any rate, outside the pages of the 'Almanach de Gotha'.

CHAPTER V

THE TOWNSMEN AND THEIR LEAGUES

THE golden age of the independent townsmen and the great leagues of cities in Germany was a short one. It fell entirely within the period starting with the twelfth and ending with the fifteenth century, and its greatest achievements belong to the thirteenth and fourteenth centuries. Before the twelfth century the development of towns in Germany was still a minor phenomenon; after the fifteenth the rise of the territorial sovereign state had effectively clipped the wings of independent urban development.

While it lasted this 'Age of the Cities' in Germany was, though different in kind, as spectacular in its results and achievements as that in Italy (beginning somewhat earlier and lasting rather longer) or in the Netherlands. It is true that the Hanseatic League and the various leagues of Rhineland cities never wielded the virtually sovereign power that certain Italian cities and city-states possessed, but, then, the Italian cities never managed to found so widespread or so effective a trading association as the Hanseatic League. They fought against and conquered one another, but they did not achieve the same degree of close and prolonged co-operation; they never had a 'Council', meeting at regular intervals. Individually the splendour and wealth of such cities as Venice, Genoa and Florence was greater than that of any German town, but collectively Italy never produced anything comparable to the Hanse. It is indeed one of the great achievements of German civilization, and not inappropriately was the great German civil airline network founded in the nineteen-twenties named *Luft-Hansa*.[1]

Just as the league of cities was a phenomenon which flourished best north of the Alps, so did it flourish better in north than in south Germany. There were reasons for this. The earlier medieval trade-routes through Germany ran from west to east across the southern edge of the north German plain, while sea-communications along the shores of the North Sea and the Baltic were always easier than land routes (especially for bulky goods) in those days. In addition, the south German cities were bedevilled in their development by being embedded in highly feudalized territories, and were subjected to much more interference by secular and religious overlords, or would-be overlords, than were most of those in the north. In the north, especially in the areas of German expansion east of the Elbe, the townsmen who settled and developed the cities very often owned the land on which they stood, and indeed the ruling oligarchies consisted usually of those 'patrician' merchant and trading families who were the owners of the plots and lots within the walls. Relatively few of the towns were 'free imperial cities' (like Goslar or Lübeck) but most of them controlled their own affairs to an extent that the typical Swabian and Franconian or Bavarian city did not. Nürnberg, for instance, was continuously being 'subjugated' and dominated by outside forces until its wealth grew so great in the fifteenth and sixteenth centuries that it had all the neighbouring territorial lords in its debt. Lübeck suffered periodic domestic upheavals,

[1] It is now (1954) about to be revived.

but these came more from dissension between different classes and strata of townsmen within her walls than from outside.

The eleventh-century German town was, it must be remembered, still a pretty rural-looking and country-minded place. Cologne, one of the largest, was said to be quite empty at harvest-time in those days, and it was not until well into the twelfth century that her population spilled over outside the lines of the walls of the small Roman city of *Colonia Claudia Agrippensis*, except in the narrow strip between those walls and the river Rhine, which had filled up in the tenth century. Lübeck, which was to become the second city of Germany and the leading city of the Hanse in the later Middle Ages, was not even founded until Henry the Lion captured the Wendish village, which stood on its site, in A.D. 1158.

During the great Interregnum in the Holy Roman Empire of the thirteenth century the Rhineland cities from Cologne to Basel had attempted to league themselves together for the protection of their common interests, and cities outside the Rhine valley as far afield as Lübeck and Regensburg had joined the Rhine League of 1254. But this league, which embraced over seventy towns and sent its own representatives to an imperial diet at Worms in 1255, soon broke down (in 1257). A year or two later the nucleus of the Hanseatic League appeared in the shape of an arrangement between several cities engaged in the Baltic trade, led by Lübeck, and this was gradually joined by more and more cities, including the free imperial cities of Cologne and Goslar, in west Germany. Cologne occupied the enviable position of being the point where two great trading routes (from the Netherlands to north-east Europe, and from the Netherlands to Switzerland and Italy) crossed, but it was too far from the centre of the activities of the Hanseatic League ever to become that league's chief city, a position that was always held by the upstart Lübeck, after the very early days when it was briefly rivalled by Visby in Gotland.

Not only did the Hanseatic League extend its trading activities westwards to Bruges (which became its most important emporium outside Germany) and to London (where the merchants of the Steelyard were very active by the thirteenth century) but also eastwards even beyond the zone of German territorial expansion, as far as Novgorod, and northwards into Scandinavia, to Bergen and beyond.[1] Here it had its warehouses and settlements and secured valuable trading privileges. Sometimes it had to fight and intrigue hard to retain these, but it held its own against the local rulers until well into the fifteenth century. Reaching its greatest power and extent by the year 1356, with upwards of one hundred towns adhering to it, the Hanseatic League (led by such cities as Lübeck, Danzig, Rostock, Riga and Reval in the Baltic area, and by Cologne, Hamburg and Emden in the North Sea region) was able to extract new privileges from the mighty city of Bruges in 1360, to conclude a very advantageous treaty with the hostile king of Denmark at Stralsund in 1370—just as they had brought the Norwegian king to heel at Tönsberg in 1294. Early in the fifteenth century the onslaughts of pirates and the continued hostility of the Scandinavian kings brought the Hanseatic League to a crisis from which it extricated itself by the truce of 1432 and the peace of 1435. But its heyday was by then over. Dissension over policy had broken out among the member-cities themselves (several of which, like Lübeck, were torn by their own internal

[1] See map on p. 39.

dissensions early in the fifteenth century) and they also were at loggerheads with foreign cities through which they had operated, notably Bruges and Novgorod. Although the League managed to browbeat Bruges into restoring their privileges, that city—its harbour silting up—had by then (1458) lost its place as the leading Netherlands port to Antwerp, while Riga (annexed by Muscovy in 1478) and Novgorod (where the Hanseatic settlement was abandoned in 1494) ceased to be within the trading orbit of the League before the fifteenth century had ended. With the decline of the Teutonic Order (and the disappearance of the powerful protection it had been able to accord to the League), after the second peace of Thorn (1466) the Hanse had to withdraw within the Empire proper, and soon only Danzig remained of its eastern outposts in Prussia or beyond. Although the League's position in England (after the riots against the Steelyard in London) and in France was restored during the reigns of Edward IV and Louis XI, this did not compensate for the loss of its North Sea and Baltic trade monopolies. In addition the new independent confederation of Switzerland and the increasingly independent Netherlands cities presented more formidable rivalry than heretofore to the League and to other German cities, while the ambitions of territorial princes within Germany reduced many of the cities to shadows of their former autonomous selves. Even the Emperor, once the great friend of cities and city leagues (though Frederick II and Charles IV in particular had resented their growing power), now turned against them. By the beginning of the sixteenth century the Hanseatic League was beginning to disintegrate—Cologne and some other cities had even seceded from it temporarily for a number of years during the fifteenth century—and its greatest days were already a memory. It lingered on even into the seventeenth century, but the new age of discovery, the concentration upon oceanic trade, and the appearance of a new type of 'national' trading company were all further nails in its coffin. But, while it lasted, it was at times (without an army, and with a navy only intermittently) the greatest power in Germany, stronger than the Emperor or any single territorial prince or Elector.

It must be repeated that nothing comparable to it ever arose in the Mediterranean area, while the cities of southern Germany, although some of them, like Augsburg and Nürnberg, did reach great importance, this was by their individual efforts and not in co-operation with others. For that reason their achievements were less widespread in their repercussions than those of the Hanseatic League. At a time when the prestige of the Empire, as such, was at a low ebb, the Hanseatic League made Germans respected throughout Europe.

CHAPTER VI

INDUSTRIAL REVOLUTION

EVERYBODY now knows what an industrial revolution is, although some have begun to doubt whether the long and often gradual process which transformed Great Britain, the prototype of such developments, from a predominantly agricultural to a predominantly industrial state really deserves the title 'revolution' at all. But if the process does not, the cumulative results certainly do. Britain in 1850 was a country different *in kind* from the Britain of 1750.

In Germany, even the process of industrialization was carried through at almost revolutionary speed. Starting about a hundred years after Britain, she had virtually caught the latter country up—and in some directions even passed her—by the year 1914. The years since 1850, and particularly since 1870, had been a period of quite feverish economic activity. Only in the United States of America was the speed of Germany's transformation matched—and later surpassed.

In her economic life Germany was, at the end of the eighteenth century (and in many respects even at the middle of the nineteenth), still the predominantly rural country, with farming in its many aspects the chief occupation of her people and source of her wealth (and manufactures on a small scale, carried on by age-old methods) that she had been in the fifteenth and sixteenth centuries. Urbanization had not advanced extensively, and the old craft-organization of the towns still persisted; some of the great merchant and banking families like the Fuggers and the Welsers in south Germany had fallen upon evil days; the mighty Hanseatic League ceased to have any corporate existence, even of a formal nature, after 1669 (when it held its last Council meeting), and its member-cities had gone their separate ways—many falling into insignificance and oblivion, but a few (like Hamburg and Danzig) flourishing, without benefit of the Hanse, as never before.

The fifteenth to the eighteenth centuries in Germany, as a whole, were indeed a period of relative economic stagnation, which of course does not mean that in certain states (such as Saxony) and cities (such as Hamburg) there were not notable advances in wealth and population, just as there were also in certain parts of sixteenth- and seventeenth-century England, though the overall picture there, too, at that time was one of a very slow change. Just as, in France, a virtually medieval economic and social system persisted until the outbreak of the great revolution of 1789, so did similar conditions continue in most parts of Germany until the Revolutionary and Napoleonic Wars, and indeed right up to the revolutions of 1848.

At some of the smaller courts and among the larger states (and in Prussia in particular) the advance out of economic stagnation began in the eighteenth century. Frederick the Great was interested in all that was going on in Britain and encouraged the managers of the various Prussian state enterprises (mines, mills, foundries and estates) to 'rationalize' their processes and introduce power-driven machinery, while in the year 1786 the Freiherr von Stein, then in charge of the Prussian state mining industry, sent over what we should call a 'working party' to visit Britain and prepare a report.

But it was not until after the defeat of Napoleon (who had thoroughly disorganized the economy of Germany by turning so much of it into a battlefield, by his economic warfare against Britain and by his repeated demands on its manpower) that the private industrial enterprises of Germany began to think about modernizing themselves and taking advantage of new inventions and technical advances. Skill and capital at first were lacking and workmen were brought over from Britain and money borrowed there by the more enterprising of the German manufacturers and mine-owners. Very few German industries were, nevertheless, on a large enough scale before the middle of the nineteenth century to profit greatly by these advances, and their foreign markets were very small—smaller indeed than they had been in some cases in the eighteenth century, before Russia adopted protective measures and raised a high tariff against German goods. The principal German manufactured exports in those days were linen and hardware, but competition from Britain in both was keen, and Sheffield was, for instance, well in advance of Solingen in its manufacturing technique. Most German industry was still on a very small scale, and the 'one-man factory', the craftsman who employed no labour and had no apprentices, was still the prevailing pattern. Where industry was on a larger scale, as was cloth-weaving in Silesia, rationalization and the introduction of machinery met with stiff resistance from workers whose traditions were those of the domestic system, and the results were unrest and unemployment of the sort portrayed so vividly by Gerhard Hauptmann in his play *The Weavers*, which refers to the period of the 1840's. Germany's struggling industrial development and export trade of course received a valuable 'shot in the arm' when the *Zollverein* (or Customs Union) of 1834 established free trade between 17 of the 39 German states, led by Prussia and containing between them over two-thirds of both the area and the population of the *Bund*.

For a number of reasons Germany's industrial revolution deviated in its nature quite widely from the British prototype, the time-element being the biggest factor in producing these differences. To begin with, the revolution in transportation came before and not after extensive industrialization and a substantial railroad and canal network therefore covered Germany long before the industrial revolution there was completed. For this reason, localization of industry, so characteristic of the British scene, was never so marked a feature of the German industrial economy. Furthermore, and perhaps this was even more important, Germany's chief deposits of workable coal were located in the areas of the greatest density of pre-industrial revolution population, so that any extensive internal migration was avoided and very few entirely new communities had to be founded. The greater urbanization of existing centres of population rather than the shift of population into new ones was therefore the prevailing trend in Germany. Very few of the centres of modern German industry were settlements without roots in the Middle Ages; villages became towns and the towns expanded, but the nucleus already existed. The social upheaval was therefore far less great than in late eighteenth- and early nineteenth-century Britain. Maps comparing Germany's population distribution in 1830 and 1930 do not exhibit any of the glaring discrepancies that are shown on similar maps for Britain in 1750 and in 1850.

Urbanization and industrialization, when it came to Germany in the second half of the nineteenth century, was very rapid indeed. The increase was relatively slow before 1870, but quite phenomenally fast after that date. Between 1815 and 1870 Germany's rural population increased by 54 per cent and her industrial population only by 70 per cent, but between 1870 and 1925 the rural increase was 26 per cent and the urban (in towns of 10,000 inhabitants or more) fully 250 per cent. In 1870 only one-twentieth of Germany's population resided in really large cities (with 100,000 inhabitants or more—of which there were eight) but by 1914 fully one-quarter lived in such large towns (and there were 48 of them!). The whole pattern of German life had been fundamentally altered in two generations. Many cities threw down their medieval walls, or incorporated suburbs outside their boundaries, only after 1870. The 'administrative sprawl' of the typical German big city falls completely within the memory of many people still living.

By 1914 Germany was Europe's largest producer of steel and chemicals, and second only to Britain in her production of machinery, textiles and coal. From the point of view of her security in time of war, as she was soon to discover, she had to pay a big price for these rapid and phenomenal industrial advances, for in 1914, also, she only produced two-thirds of the food and animal foodstuffs that she consumed. Her supreme self-confidence in her ability to knock out her opponents in 1914 in a short war led her to neglect this lack of balance in her economy until it was too late, and the terrible turnip-winters of 1917 and 1918 were part of the price that she had to pay. The ill-nourished urban children of those years were to become the physically and mentally maladjusted dupes who flocked to the pied-piper death-dance of Adolf Hitler twenty years later. The German industrial revolution, as it ran its course after 1871, was, in fact, much more suited to the needs of the 'satiated state' which Bismarck claimed he had created in that year. Germany's later bid for colonies did not disturb that pattern, for primarily it sought to secure for her control over overseas markets and sources of raw material commensurate with her industrial strength and needs at home, but her return to a policy of expansion in Europe, her desire to incorporate or dominate every corner of that continent where the German tongue was spoken or outpost of German culture existed, demanded a different pattern, and the *Autarky*, which Hitler, Schacht and their associates attempted feverishly to create in the nineteen-thirties, to meet this new need or obsession, was started too late.

CHAPTER VII

POPULATION PROBLEMS

DEMOGRAPHERS continue to quarrel quite viciously concerning the size of the population of medieval Europe, but the most convincing estimates appear to put the population of Germany at between 4 and 5 million in the year A.D. 500, towards the end of the great *Völkerwanderung*, and to consider that it had increased about threefold, to at least 12 million, by the year A.D. 1300—an average increase of around a million for every century.

In the fourteenth century, as everywhere else in Europe, this steady though unspectacular growth received a severe setback through the effects of the Black Death and other plagues and famines of the period, and it is thought that Germany's population was reduced to no more than 8 million by A.D. 1350. It was perhaps up to at least 12 million again by A.D. 1500. The figure of 20 million in 1600 seems rather more reliable, but then there was another serious setback caused by the devastations and loss of civilian life in the Thirty Years War (A.D. 1618–48). The effects of the Thirty Years War have in the past been somewhat exaggerated, some estimates having claimed a reduction of the population by 1650 down to as low as 8 million again. A more plausible figure is 14 million, which is itself bad enough, for it means that fully one-third of Germany's population was wiped out in those thirty years.

By A.D. 1700 the figure had risen again to about

15 million, or to the level that had been reached at the end of the Middle Ages. The ups and downs of over two centuries had thus only served to cancel each other out, and these two centuries were therefore not in any way a period of population-pressure in the towns or the countryside. Little new building was needed, except for improvement and replacement, and very few new settlements and urban centres were founded. Up to a little before the outbreak of the Thirty Years War it was a period of increasing wealth and rising standards of living, especially in the towns, and, after the failure of the peasant uprisings in the early sixteenth century, and the ending of the Reformation wars soon after its middle, a distinct era of prosperity was enjoyed corresponding in time and mood to the Elizabethan age in England, though, like the latter, it was not without its serious economic and population problems. The 'Sturdy Beggar' was, for instance, a German as well as an English social phenomenon.

England was to escape the horrors inflicted upon the people of Germany and Bohemia by the Thirty Years War, and her own Civil War, contemporaneous with the concluding years of the former, caused by contrast no very great disturbance to ordinary civil life, and only a negligible number of civilian casualties. In Germany a period of economic decline had already begun to set in before 1618, and although the Thirty Years War greatly accentuated the depression that followed, it would probably have been a period of retrogression, though not necessarily of declining population, even if the war had not happened.

After 1650 emigration out of Germany began again on a large scale, for even the reduced population was too large for the depleted economy and resources of the country at that time. This emigration went both to the new areas of south-east Europe that the Habsburgs (assisted by many Thirty Years War veterans in their armies) were freeing from the Ottoman Turks (whose last great incursion into central Europe was the unsuccessful attack on Vienna in 1683) and overseas to the new colonial areas, especially those under British sovereignty in North America. No German state at this time managed to secure territory in North America, so there was not a natural stream of emigration from the homeland to a New Brandenburg, a Nova Austria or a New Saxony or Palatinate, such as there was from neighbouring lands to New England, New Spain, New France, New Amsterdam or Nova Scotia, but the foundation of Pennsylvania in 1683, as a colony open to the oppressed and the persecuted of all nations, acted as a magnet to the peoples of the many depressed areas of western Germany, especially after Louis XIV had carried fire and sword into the Palatinate and across the Rhine again and yet again, culminating in the holocaust of A.D. 1689 when, for instance, the great palace and castle and indeed the whole town of Heidelberg (then capital of the Elector of the Palatinate) went up in flames.

By the year A.D. 1700 Germany's population was, as has been seen, back to about 15 million again, and this marked the beginning of a long period of increase that was not broken until the great wars of the twentieth century and the reductions in territory and population caused by these. The wars of the eighteenth century and the Revolutionary and Napoleonic wars, with all their drain on Germany's manpower, did not cause any actual depopulation, while the nineteenth century, after 1815, was an era of long periods of peace interrupted briefly (in 1848, in 1859, in 1866 and in 1870, for instance) by several very short and relatively non-destructive wars.

The eighteenth century, though that great stimulus to population-increase, the Industrial and Commercial Revolution, had not yet reached Germany, was one of steadily and, in some states, spectacularly increasing population. Prussia, for instance (gaining new territories all the while for her people to exploit), reached a population of 6 million by the year 1800, of whom fully 1 million were immigrants, or the descendants of immigrants, brought in by the policy pursued by Prussia's rulers between 1640 and 1786. By the year 1815 Germany's population (in the 39 states of the *Bund*) was approximately 25 million, or nearly twice what it had been just over a century earlier. This was the greatest rate of increase in all of Germany's history, and provided her with the mass of potential soldiers and industrial workers which was necessary for her as the world-power she was to become in the nineteenth century. A people of 25 million was a very considerable proportion of the whole population of Europe in 1815. It was far larger than that of the British Isles and nearly as big as that of France. Indeed, the big feature of the demographic history of Europe in the nineteenth century was the way in which Germany passed and left France far behind in size of population. In 1830 France, with 31 million, probably still just held the lead; by 1930 France had only 41 to Germany's 63 million.

The increase was achieved despite the great drain of resumed emigration overseas after 1815, which took fully 6 million of Germany's inhabitants away during the hundred years that followed—at least $5\frac{1}{2}$ million of these going to the United States of America. Emigration for religious reasons (such a potent cause in the seventeenth and eighteenth centuries) had virtually ceased —though the Old Lutherans, who went to Wisconsin and elsewhere in the 1840's, were an exception—but rural over-population in the divided-up farmsteads of south and west Germany, the desire everywhere to escape conscription and political repression (especially in the years immediately after 1848), and many other reasons, still impelled Germans to seek asylum and a fuller life overseas.[1]

The really phenomenal increase in modern Germany's population came, as has already been noticed, only after unification was achieved in 1871 and after the Industrial Revolution was (by that time) well under way. A population of 25 million in 1815 advanced to 36 million by 1855, to 41 million by 1871, to 56 million by 1900 and to 64 million by 1910. The increase between 1871 and 1910 was thus over 50 per cent. An increasing birth-rate (which did not begin to decline until after 1914) and a falling death-rate (down to 20 per thousand by 1900) helped to contribute to this remarkable situation. By 1914 also, two-fifths of all Germany's workers were in industry, and nearly half of her population lived in her larger towns and cities.

If Germany could have kept out of long-drawn-out major wars in the first half of the twentieth century (as she did under the wiser statesmanship of Bismarck in the latter half of the nineteenth) there is no telling how rapidly her population would have continued to increase. As it was, it was down to under 61 million again by 1921 (and her territory was reduced as a result of the First World War by some 26,000 square miles, or by about one-seventh). By 1935 the 1910 figures of nearly 65 million had been exceeded once more (with just 66 million) in the reduced area, and by 1939 the annexation of Austria and other territories had brought 'Greater

[1] See further pp. 179–189.

Germany' to just on 80 million. By the first post-war census of 1946 it was (in a territory now reduced by over one-third) down to 66 million once again.

Meanwhile, in the 1930's, the birth-rate had begun to fall (the net reproduction rate was down to 0·76 by 1933, and even the Nazis only brought it, by their many propaganda drives and bounties for large families, up to parity by 1939) and even without the losses of population and territory in World War II, population stability and decline might have been reached in Germany by the year 1955, or at the latest by 1970. The situation in the years immediately succeeding that war was very much confused by the incursion of over 10 million foreign workers (not all of whom returned home) into Germany during the war, and by the arrival of over 12 million refugees from the lost eastern territories after the war ended or in its concluding stages. The much reduced post-war Germany had, in all four zones of occupation in the year 1953, a total population of some 64 million, of whom fully 48 million resided in the West German Republic. The fluctuations in Germany's population in the twentieth century, after the steady and at times rapid advance of the eighteenth and nineteenth, have thus been very remarkable, and have introduced a factor of instability into the life of that country which has made economic and social planning, though even more essential than before, almost insuperably difficult. No other large country of the western world has witnessed such demographic vicissitudes during the past hundred years.

MAP 9. GERMANY: ZONES OF OCCUPATION, 1945

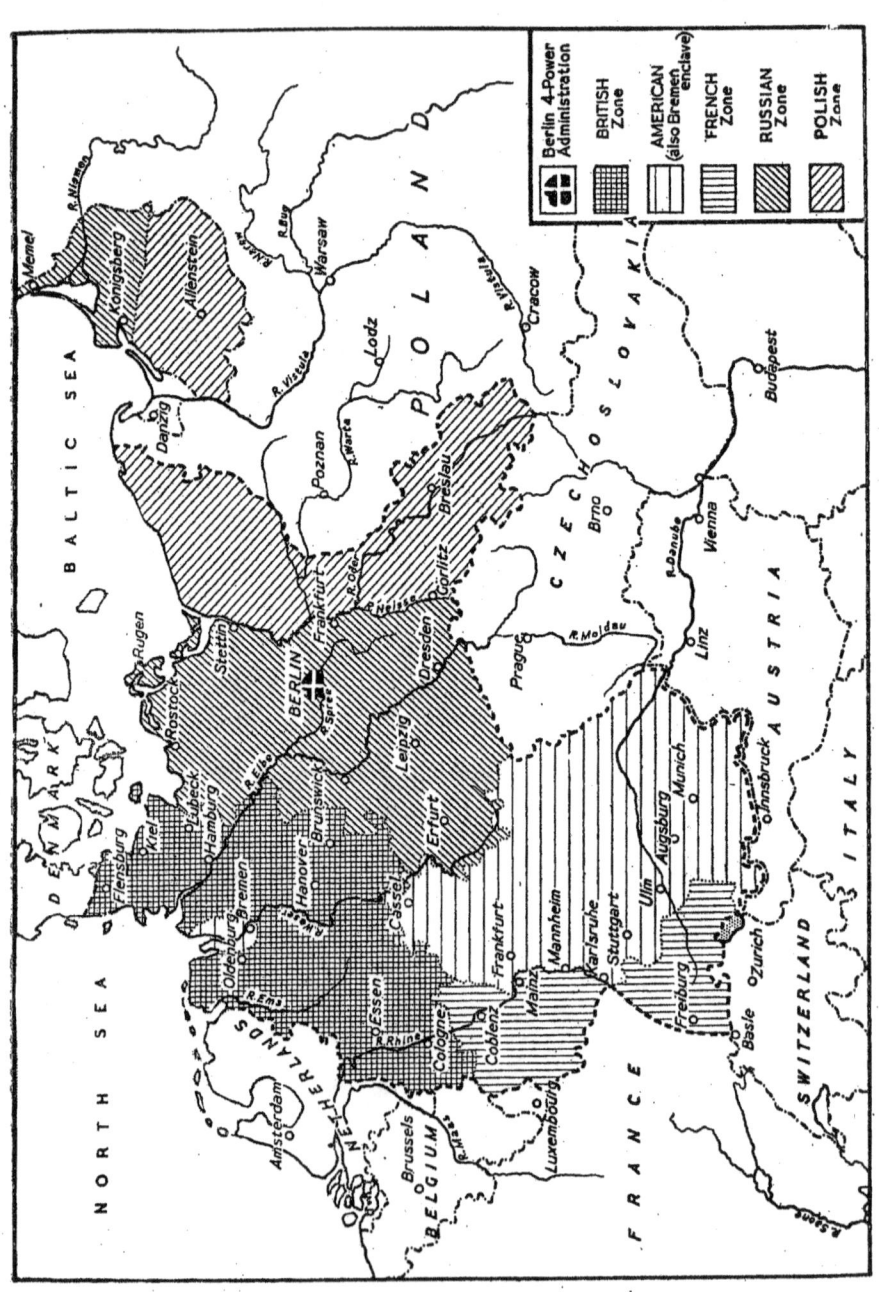

Part III   *The States of Germany*

CHAPTER I

EAST AND WEST GERMANY SINCE 1945

GERMANY had only one decade of 'enjoyment' of her first complete unification, achieved through the elimination by *Gleichschaltung* of the powers and local autonomy of the separate provinces (or *Länder*) by Adolf Hitler in the middle 1930's. On 7 May, 1945, her enemies received Germany's unconditional surrender and the *Reich*, incompletely unified by Bismarck in 1871 and, at last, fully unified by Hitler after 1933, again disappeared entirely, just as the much more shadowy Holy Roman *Reich* had disappeared in 1806. It was no longer correct, after the unconditional surrender, to speak of 'Germany' as a political entity at all. After the abortive 'succession' government of Admiral Dönitz had been rounded up in Schleswig-Holstein, there was no longer a central administration or a head of the state, or a Chancellor. The four occupying powers dealt severally and piecemeal with whatever local personalities and bodies they chose to recognize—or make use of. Anybody not obviously tainted with Nazi affiliations, and not on a black list, tended to have authority—or at least responsibility—thrust upon him. The Germans in the four zones of occupation found themselves separated by the arbitrary boundaries of these zones as if they were in different countries. Even within each zone there was no administrative cohesion for a long time between the new *Länder* (by no means always coinciding with the former

Länder of the Weimar Republic) into which the conquerors divided it. Thus, in the British zone, the *Land* of North Rhine-Westphalia, centred on Düsseldorf, was administered quite separately from the neighbouring *Land* of Lower Saxony, centred on Hanover. It was as if Germany was back to the days of the 39 separate states of 1814, but without a *Bund* to bind them even loosely together—and none of these petty states had a German prince or governor at its head, but, instead, a foreign general or official.

Gradually an inter-*Land* administration was worked out in each separate zone, and then came (in and after 1947) the administrative *rapprochement* of the British and American zones, with which the French zone was somewhat tardily and reluctantly—and never very completely—integrated. The Soviet zone was from the beginning a law unto itself, and after the Berlin blockade and the coming of the 'cold war' in 1948 had drawn an iron curtain between it and the three western zones, it was progressively 'unified' by the suppression of the informal autonomy that had existed in the *Länder* of Saxony, Thuringia, Brandenburg, Mecklenburg and Saxony-Anhalt which had comprised it. Finally, in July 1952, the East German (Soviet zone) *Länder* were formally abolished. West Germany remained the Federal Republic of nine separate *Länder*, which had been recognized by the three western occupying powers in 1949, and their control was made progressively less strict under the civil High Commission established at Bonn (the federal capital) to succeed the purely military government that had been set up in 1945.

Thus, in the year 1954, Germany still had not regained her international position as a fully sovereign power, leave alone her recently found unity. Hitler's

'Greater Germany' had disappeared almost as soon as it had been created; the eastern province so long disputed with the Poles were now in Polish hands, and, in the eyes of Poles and Russians at least, were permanently alienated from Germany; Austria was again an independent state (though itself still under a fourfold occupation); the disputed borderlands in the west—Alsace, Lorraine, Eupen and Malmedy were outside Germany once more; the Saarland, the ultimate fate of which had yet to be decided, was still firmly in French hands. It looked as if the clock of German unification had been put back by at least a thousand years. Neither the West German Republic of Conrad Adenauer and Theodor Heuss nor the East German People's Republic of Otto Grotewohl and Wilhelm Pieck was as complete a 'Germany' as that over which Henry the Fowler had held sway a full millenium earlier. Berlin, the former capital of Prussia and of the Hohenzollern-Bismarckian Empire, of the Weimar Republic and of Hitler's Third Reich, was no longer a capital or a focus of anything, except perhaps of the great sense of political frustration that hung over all Germans. Unity, for which Germans had so long striven, seemed as far away as ever for them as they entered the second half of the twentieth century. How did it come about that a politically unified state of 'Germany' always seemed to vanish again the moment it was within the grasp of its peoples? An examination in reversed historical order of the various attempts to create a unified Germany may help to answer this question.

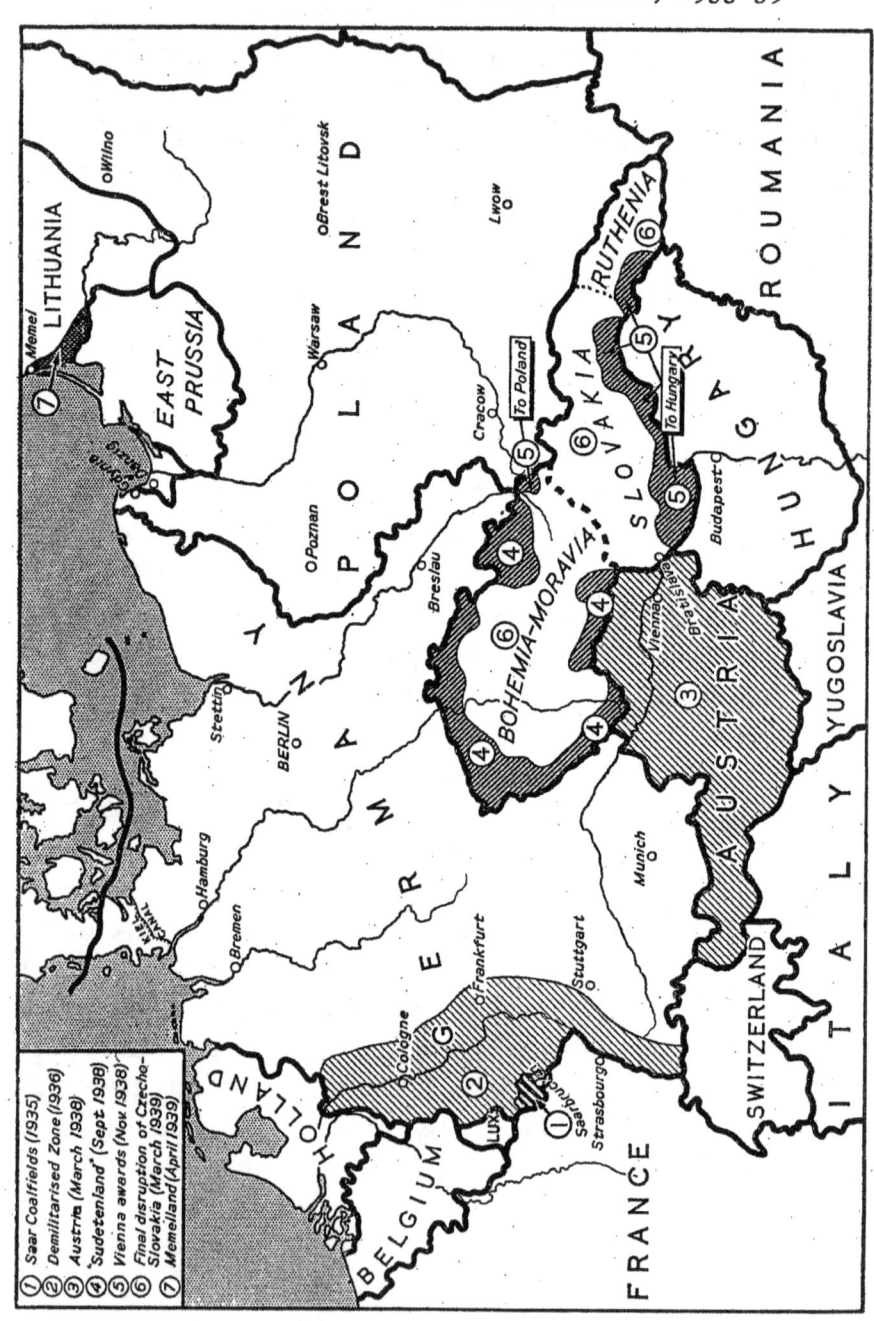

CHAPTER II

THE NAZI STATE:
HITLER'S 'GREATER GERMANY'

WE are not concerned here with the personality or the diplomacy of Adolf Hitler, but with the kind of state he brought into existence in Germany during his twelve brief years of virtual dictatorship between 1933 and 1945. Under Hitler Germany achieved her most complete unification and her widest territorial expansion, and she was also brought to the most complete political disintegration of all her history since the Dark Ages, when his Third Reich fell to pieces. Even during the great interregnum which followed the end of the Hohenstauffen dynasty in A.D. 1256 Germany was not so completely submerged as a political entity as she was after 7 May, 1945.

Hitler found Germany a truly federal state with the classic division of powers between the central and the *Land* (or state) governments very completely worked out in accordance with the main features of the great prototype of modern federal constitutions, that of the United States of America. He turned Germany into the most completely unitary state in Europe, more unitary than the Revolution of 1789 and Napoleon had made France, much more unitary than Great Britain, far more unitary, of course, than Switzerland. He had already declared war upon the federal principle adopted somewhat incompletely by Bismarck and much more logically by the makers of the Weimar Republic of 1919, when he wrote in *Mein Kampf* that 'We can have no separate states within the nation', and thus it was not surprising that, within a month or so of seizing power in Germany, he took away from the *Länder* (on 31 March, 1933) all their legislative powers and suspended the functions of their elected assemblies. A week later (on 7 April) he placed a regent (or *Staathalter*) nominated by himself in charge of the administration of each *Land*, himself becoming *Staathalter* in Prussia. Prussia, which had tended to dominate the Hohenzollern-Bismarckian administration, and had still remained very powerful under the Weimar republic, was now reduced by Hitler to impotence along with all the other *Länder*. The *Staathalter* acted as it were as official receivers on behalf of the *Reich*, while the affairs of the *Länder* in liquidation were being wound up. Within a very short time all traces of the old provincial autonomy of the *Länder*, and of the *Staaten* of the Bismarckian Empire which had preceded them, had disappeared, except as a memory, in the minds of their inhabitants and former officials, who were now called upon to follow without question the star of 'One *Reich*, one people, one leader'.

It was almost unnecessary after this for Hitler to abolish (as he did in 1934) the representative assemblies in the former *Länder*, and the *Reichsrat* or federal second chamber. The *Reichstag* or central lower house was allowed to remain as a rubber-stamp assembly, its all-Nazi membership hand-picked by the party leadership to yell 'Ja!' and 'Heil!' at the word of command.

Into this completely unified *Reich* with all local autonomy pulverized (not merely that of the states or *Länder* but that of the purely local authorities, such as the *Kreise*, as well), Austria was absorbed as an integral

MAP II. GERMANY'S GREATEST MODERN EXPANSION, 1942

part of Germany after the *Anschluss* of March 1938 and so was the 'Sudetenland', taken from Czechoslovakia by the terms of the Munich settlement of September 1938. Hitler's 'Big (or greater) Germany', unified in a way that the 'Little (or lesser) Germany' of Bismarck had never been, was in existence—and all this had been achieved by means short of an outright military attack upon any of Germany's neighbours. The next stages were not to be so easy. Poland was occupied up to the 'line of demarkation' between German and Soviet occupying forces in September 1939 only after she had been invaded; Alsace and Lorraine and Eupen and Malmedy were only wrested back after the defeat of France and Belgium in the *Blitzkrieg* of the summer of 1940; the 'General Government' of eastern Poland and the Russian Ukraine could only be set up after the Soviet Union had been attacked in 1941. But by 1942 the frontiers of 'Greater Germany' were truly impressive; they stretched from the Meuse to Bessarabia, from Memel almost to Zagreb. They incorporated as subject provinces not only Poland but Bohemia and Moravia, while nominally outside Greater Germany the satellite states of Slovakia and Croatia constituted servile hangers-on of Hitler's *Reich* only slightly less in his toils than the formally annexed territories.

The 'General Government' of Poland and the 'Protectorate' of Bohemia-Moravia were administered for the sake of convenience through Hitler's viceroys Rosenberg and Neurath, but they had even less local autonomy than the former *Länder* of Germany and Austria. Everything was reduced to a common level. This indeed was 'Unification' for Germany—but at the price of all her cherished local traditions and provincial ways of life, and at the expense of the freedom and in some cases the separate national existences of neighbouring peoples who lived in what the Nazis considered to be her 'Lebensraum', as well as at the cost of the lives of millions of the minority groups (such as the Jews) whom they chose to slaughter rather than to assimilate.

Never in all their history since the barbarian invasions had the Germans been so hated and feared in Europe as Hitler and his henchmen made them in the twelve short years ending in 1945.

CHAPTER III
THE WEIMAR REPUBLIC

GERMANY's defeat of 1918 destroyed the Second Reich created by Bismarck to the extent that it drove the Hohenzollern emperor and all the kings and grand dukes off their thrones in the states which had made up the federalized empire of 1871, but it did not destroy the unity which had then been achieved. Indeed, the Republic set up in 1919 was, if anything, a step—or at least a half step—nearer to the unitary state Bismarck had been unable to create. It did not prove possible (as Dr. Hugo Preuss, the drafter of the Weimar Constitution, had hoped) to break up Prussia into a number of separate states, and thus destroy her dominating position in the *Reich*, but she was at least not so powerful in the Weimar Republic as she had been in the empire of 1871. There was also a certain amount of administrative tidying up when the *Staaten* of the Second Reich became the *Länder* of the Weimar Republic. For instance a new *Land* of Thuringia was created out of seven former diminutive *Staaten* in central Germany—one of them being the famous little Grand Duchy of Saxe-Weimar where Goethe had served as minister a century before.

The principal change in the form of the German nation-state made in 1919 was that the somewhat illogical federalism of Bismarck (based upon opportunism and compromise—especially with regard to the powers 'reserved' by the three southern states of

MAP 12. GERMANY BEFORE AND AFTER WORLD WAR I

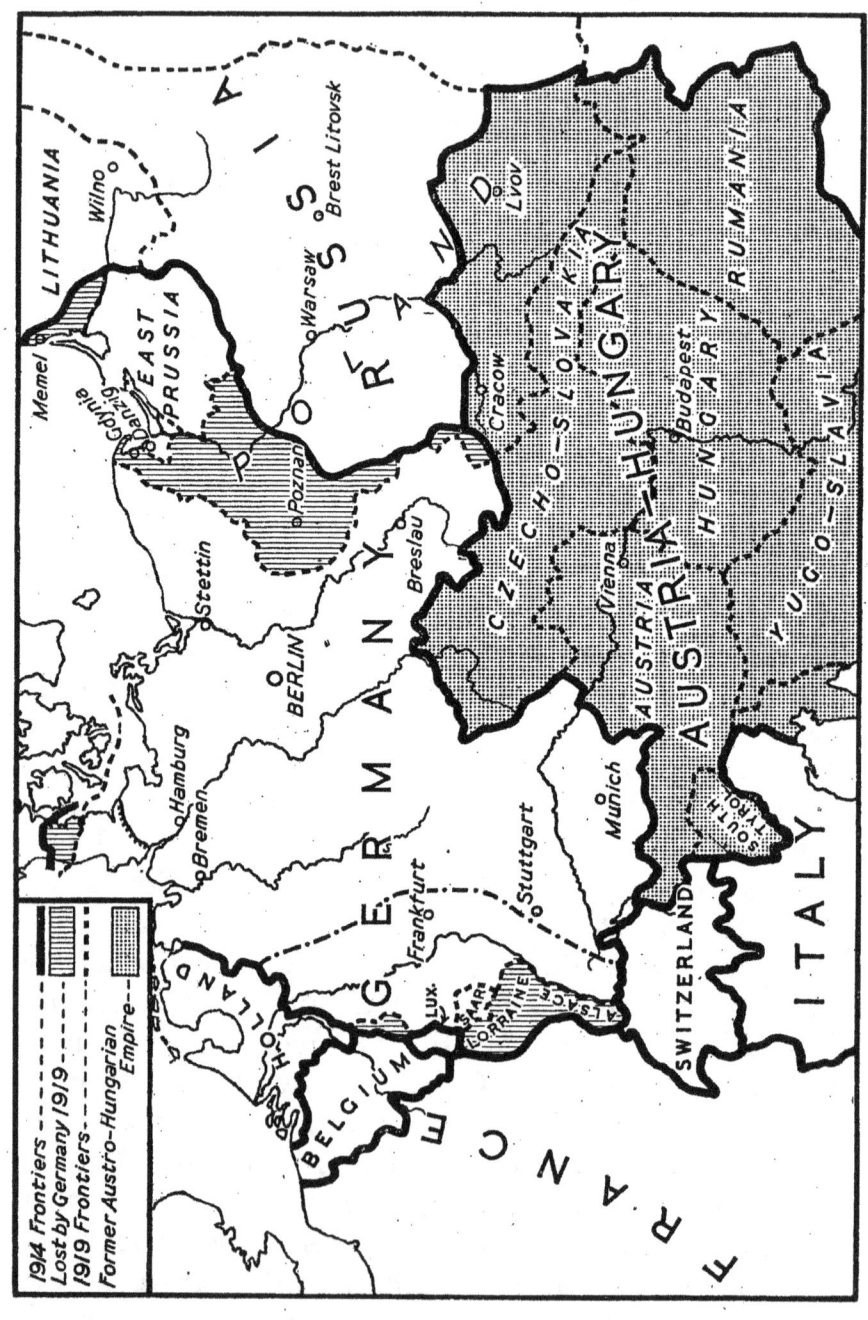

Bavaria, Baden and Württemberg) was now replaced by the ultra-logical and very doctrinaire federal system devised by Hugo Preuss. Drawing heavily upon the abortive Frankfurt Constitution of 1849 (which in its turn had owed much to the United States Constitution of 1787) the Weimar Constitution of 1919 re-defined the sphere of the central government and made it much broader than in 1867 and 1871, though residual powers still stayed with the *Länder*. There was, nevertheless, no question of the right of secession being left to the *Länder*, and perhaps the makers of the Weimar Constitution had in mind (as had Bismarck before them) the constitutional struggle in the United States which had culminated in the Civil War. *Reich* law was declared to be supreme and to prevail over territorial law, the Supreme Court of the country deciding in disputed cases. In addition to this very obvious debt to the United States, the principles of cabinet government were borrowed from Britain and direct democracy from Switzerland. There was to be no sovereign executive or sovereign parliament, for the President (elected directly for a term of seven years) and the *Reichstag* occupied positions (theoretically at least) of equal importance; both were representative of the sovereign people; each acted as a counterpoise to the other. The federal upper house, or *Reichsrat* (composed, as had been the old Bismarckian *Bundesrat*, of representatives of the governments of the memberstates) was definitely made a subordinate body and its part in legislation was little more than subsidiary.

As befitted a country which had been a pioneer in social and economic legislation under the Hohenzollern Empire, the German Republic made special provision for the regulation of economic life. In this connection it was more frankly experimental and original than in purely political matters. Thus both the right and the duty to work were affirmed (article 163 of the Weimar Constitution); labour was placed under the special protection of the *Reich*; a 'decent standard of living' was asserted to be of primary importance; and a federal economic council (in addition to local workers' and employers' councils) was to be set up.

The Weimar Constitution was full of good ideas and even fuller of good intentions (such as the federal economic council which never actually amounted to anything) and it failed less because it was a bad constitution than because it was adopted in the shadow of defeat and operated in the midst of very hard times—first the inflation of the early 1920's and then (after the brief 'honeymoon period' of Locarno and Stresemann between 1925 and 1929) the depression of the early 1930's. All the cards were stacked against it, and Hitler was able to sweep it (or as much as he desired of it) away overnight in 1933.

In the long striving for a truly unified Germany the Weimar period and the Weimar Constitution occupied a significant place and performed an important part. It went beyond the Frankfurt Constitution of 1849 and far beyond the Bismarckian constitution of 1871 (with its concessions to particularist feeling and the predominance it gave to Prussia). It was more than a purely verbal change that the *Staaten* of 1871 became *Länder*—whose boundaries could be changed without their own consent and whose form of government had to be republican—in 1919. It has been well said that 'The *Reich* which Bismarck forged was a federal union of hitherto sovereign states; the new *Reich* was the political organization of a single people, subsidiarily divided into largely autonomous political units to which the name state might or might not be given.'

After 1919 Germans who had been disappointed that a more truly unitary state had not been created at Weimar, attempted from time to time to reform the republican constitution in a unitary direction, or else to devise informal administrative machinery that would draw its several parts more closely together. Nothing as thoroughgoing as the amalgamation of several small territories into a new *Land* of reasonable size (as had happened when Thuringia came into being) was achieved, although a conference of *Länder* governments held in 1928 proposed a number of equally far-reaching reforms, including the formation of 21 new *Länder* (in place of the existing 17) equal in size and population with the major provinces of Prussia ranking as *Länder* along with the rest. An alternative plan (sponsored by the then Reich-Chancellor, Dr. Luther) would have permitted Prussia to remain as one *Land*, and indeed would have absorbed several of the smaller *Länder* within Prussia, leaving only Thuringia, Mecklenburg, Hessen, Hamburg and Bremen, together with the larger southern states of Saxony, Bavaria, Baden and Württemberg as separate *Länder*. Neither of these schemes had come to anything before the Nazis, in and after 1933, adopted more radical solutions, using much more ruthless methods than those proposed by the democrats of the 1920's.

CHAPTER IV

THE HOHENZOLLERN EMPIRE: BISMARCK'S 'LESSER GERMANY'

THE 'Second German Reich'—as it is sometimes called—created by Bismarck in 1871 was the product partly of consolidation and partly of federation. It was achieved in two bites, the North German Confederation of 1867 and the Empire of 1871, but the constitutions of these two composite states were in all essentials identical. The 'President' of the Confederation became 'Emperor' four years later, when its boundaries were extended to comprehend the German states south of the Main river, though Austria was still excluded.

The Hohenzollern Empire did not give to Germany either the unity or the extent that the coming into force of the Frankfurt constitution of 1849 would have secured for her, but it was a distinct step forward from the chronically disarticulated *Bund* of 1815. National legislation was made superior to state laws within the sphere of the federal authority, and equal and uniform civil rights were given to all Germans living within the bounds of the empire. The country was to have one customs system, one postal system and one army (with minor concessions to particularist feeling in Bremen and Hamburg in 1867 and in Bavaria, Württemberg and Baden in 1871) in addition to one foreign policy and one foreign office, none of which the *Bund* of 1815 had possessed. Not even Prussia

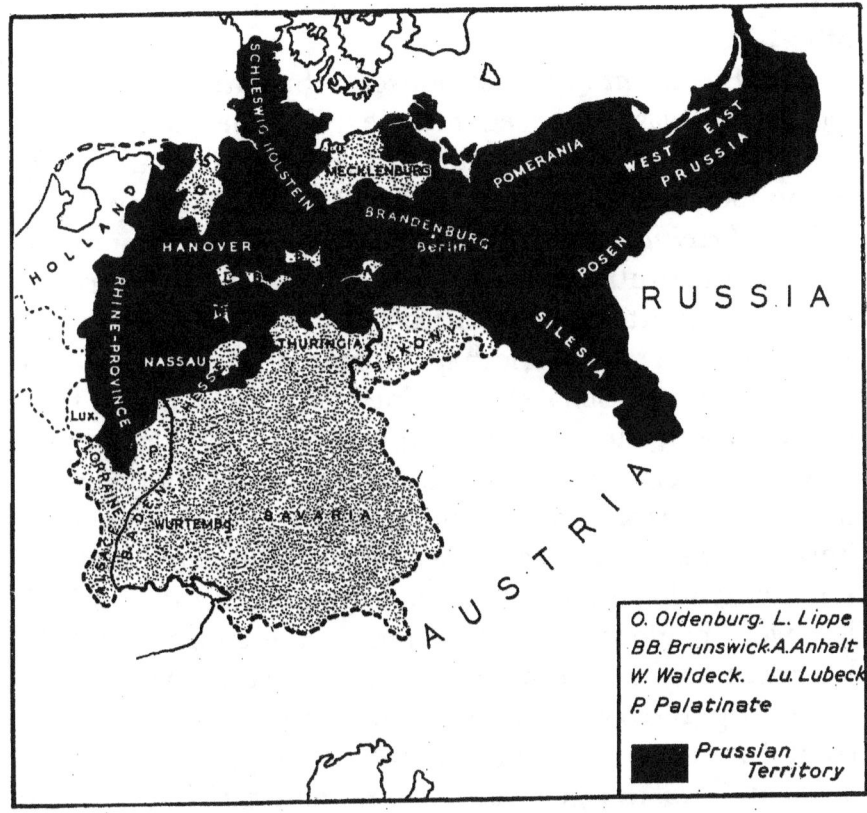

MAP 13. BISMARCK'S UNITED GERMANY, 1871–1918

was to continue to send her separate ambassadors abroad.

Bismarck admitted the principle of universal manhood suffrage for elections to the *Reichstag* or lower house of the national legislature (although the old illiberal three-class franchise of 1850 remained in force in Prussia) but he was careful not to let responsible self-government accompany this wide measure of representative government. The Chancellor, or prime minister, of the *Reich* was appointed by the Emperor and responsible to him alone, and was not dependent on the support of a majority in the *Reichstag* for continuing in office.

The *Bundesrat* or upper house of the national German legislature was supposed to safeguard the particularist traditions of the separate states of the Bismarckian *Reich*, but in fact it came to be overshadowed by the popularly elected *Reichstag* and never played a really significant part in the constitutional history of the *Reich*. Its foreign affairs committee (insisted upon by the south German states in 1871, and perhaps inspired by that of the United States Senate) remained inactive, while first Bismarck and, later on, the Emperor William II sought to treat the foreign policy of the *Reich* as a strictly personal matter. Indeed, in other directions too, the particularist implications of the second *Reich* were blunted in practice. Unitary tendencies were many. Commercial and criminal law were made uniform throughout the country and so later was civil law; a national supreme court was set up at Leipzig; the courts and legal procedure were standardized; Bremen and Hamburg were brought, by mutual consent, into the general customs and tariff system in 1888; a *Reich* colonial office was created when Germany belatedly became a colonial power; all Bismarck's spectacular new social insurance legislation was administered nationally; and a federal income-tax law was passed in 1913.

By 1914 the German *Reich* was not yet as tightly knit a federal state as the United States of America or Switzerland or as the Frankfurt constitution would have made it at one stroke in 1849, but it was a great and powerful country with a strong sense of national cohesion and an enormous pride in its achievements since 1870. The petty particularism of the days of the old *Bund* was dead. Even the resentment in some areas (such as

Hanover) at the way in which unification had been achieved by Prussia at their expense in the sixties, was dying. Germany had never before been so unified, or so powerful, as on the day she invaded Belgium in August 1914.

CHAPTER V

THE PLAN FOR GERMAN UNITY OF 1848-49

A LOT of nonsense has been written about the German revolutions—for there were several quite separate ones—of ‹1848 and 1849, and of the ineffectiveness of the 'Professors' Parliament' that met in Frankfurt-am-Main on 18 May, 1848 to devise a national and democratic constitution for all Germany, including Austria. Actually the Parliament (like almost every other parliament and national assembly) was dominated by judges and lawyers rather than by professors, and the constitution it produced had many excellent features, quite a few of which were to be borrowed by Bismarck in 1867 and in 1871 and also by the Weimar constitution-makers of 1919. What was fatal to the success of the work of the Parliament was the leisurely way in which it proceeded to complete the constitution (taking nearly a year, compared with the thirteen days required a year later by the framers of the first constitution of the state of California at Monterey, and the seven weeks duration of the Philadelphia Convention of 1787), the way in which the Parliament allowed itself to be sidetracked from its early liberalism to indulge in rodomontades of German chauvinism (against Denmark, Poland, the Slavs generally, the French, and almost everybody else in turn), and the extent to which the deference of the members of the Parliament towards the King of Prussia caused them to be manœuvred into letting him sabotage it completely when they offered him the position of head of the new German federal state that the constitution would have set up.

The Frankfurt Parliament itself, democratically elected in all the states of the German *Bund*, including Austria, rather put the cart before the horse by wasting precious months in elaborating a Declaration of the Rights of the German People (instead of adding one to their already completed constitution as a sort of appendix, as did the Americans) but when they did get down to the details of a federal constitution for all of Germany they showed much political wisdom and displayed considerable knowledge of all the best examples from which they might learn. In many respects they improved upon the constitution of the United States of America, and they watched with profit the parallel constitution-making of the Swiss that was going on at the same time. Disappointed by the refusal of the Czechs to send delegates to Frankfurt and by the early withdrawal of the Austrian representatives (after they had played a prominent part in the opening deliberations of the Parliament and provided, in Anton von Schmerling, a prime minister for the Frankfurt provisional government and, in the Archduke John, a provisional 'head of state'), the makers of the Frankfurt constitution had to concentrate not only on the purely German lands of the former *Bund*, but upon a 'lesser Germany' excluding *all* the crown-lands of the Habsburg Empire—even German-Austria. This truncation of their task might have daunted a less determined or less dedicated group of patriots, who had also to suffer the increasingly active opposition (culminating in an armed rebellion in Baden) of the left-wing republicans led by Friedrich Hecker, and the equally damaging polemical attacks of the extreme left-wing socialists and communists led by Karl Marx in Cologne. But they persisted in their task even when the tide of revolution had turned against them and reaction had set in again almost everywhere. The constitution they published in March 1849 was still-born, but had they finished it in the autumn (or preferably the summer) of 1848, it might have gone into force and given to 'Lesser Germany' unification on a satisfactory and dignified basis a full generation before Bismarck imposed it upon her by methods 'not of speechifying and majorities, but of blood and iron'. Had there been no Bismarckian-type unification there might have been no Wilhelmian blundering into a First World War, or Hitlerian engineering into a Second World War, in the twentieth century. The failure of the Frankfurt Constitution to go into force was one of the great tragedies of German—and of European—history.

CHAPTER VI

THE GERMAN *BUND* OF 1815-66

IF the Confederation of the Rhine was Napoleon's attempt to solve the German problem in his own interests —and those of France—the German *Bund* or Confederation of 1815 was the attempt of Prince Metternich to put it on ice, not so much solving it in Austria's favour as preserving what may be called the *status quo post bellum*. Nobody, least of all Metternich (who himself had collaborated with Napoleon during the uneasy Austro-French alliance following the marriage of the Emperor with the Archduchess Maria Louisa), sought to restore the separate sovereignties of the four hundred or so states into which Germany had still been divided in 1789, but he did aim to check the advance of liberal institutions in the thirty-nine much larger states (in most cases) into which these four hundred had been welded by the events of the Revolutionary and Napoleonic era. By creating a sort of permanent conference of ambassadors, under the perpetual chairmanship of the Austrian delegate, he also aimed to keep an eye upon German affairs generally, and in particular to watch that Prussia did not exploit her new prestige due to her leading part in the 'Liberation' and her acquisition of fresh territories in western Germany (notably the Rhine provinces) to secure a dominating position among the German states, a prerogative which Metternich regarded as belonging to Austria.

110   THE STATES OF GERMANY

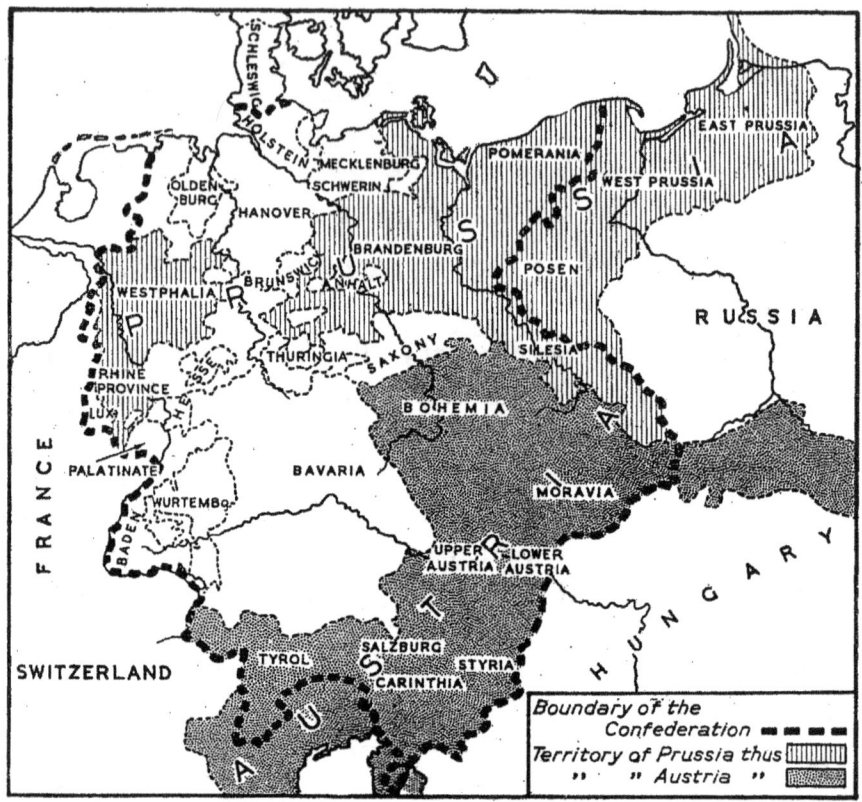

MAP 14.   THE GERMAN *Bund* OF 1815

This battle on two fronts, against liberalism and against Prussia at the same time, was ultimately to prove too much for the strength of Austria and even for the political adroitness of Metternich, but for some thirty years it was more or less successful, and after the interlude of the 1848 revolutionary movement (which swept Metternich from the scene) had ended, the same policy was continued in the hands of other Austrian statesmen until their humiliation at the hands of Bismarck and the breaking up of the *Bund* in 1866. The struggle against Prussia was then abandoned, but the fight against liberalism continued.

Thus the *Bund* of 1815 acted as an instrument to

prolong artificially, to and beyond the middle of the nineteenth century, that position of leadership in Germany which Austria had held by right—but against growing *de facto* Prussian competition—up to the formal demise of the Holy Roman Empire in 1806. The *Bundesakte* of 1815 was therefore less a constitution for Germany than a device, an elaborate piece of mechanism, for securing Austria's ends. The *Bundesakte*, in fact, possessed about all the faults that might render a constitution for a German nation utterly useless.

The five-sixths of the population of the Germany of 1815 that lived in the seven largest states were allotted only twenty-seven votes in the *Bundestag*, or Diet of the *Bund*, while the remaining one-sixth of the population (in the smaller states) had forty-two votes—and there was no second chamber, such as existed in the United States of America, to redress the balance in favour of the larger states. In addition to this, all matters of importance and anything involving modification of the fundamental law of the *Bund* was subject to the veto of any single member-state. Austria could thus prevent any changes without even having to bother to rally the smaller states behind her. It has well been said that, by this device, 'A new Polish Diet was founded; a permanent obstacle was imposed against the legislative development of the future German United States; the party of reform was forced into the paths of revolution.'

CHAPTER VII

NAPOLEON'S 'THIRD GERMANY': THE CONFEDERATION OF THE RHINE

THE importance of the impact of the French Revolution upon Germany is discussed elsewhere.[1] The decade of Napoleon Bonaparte's domination over Europe also saw very great changes in the state and states of Germany. Indeed, G. P. Gooch has claimed that 'few people advanced so far in so short a time as the Germans between 1789 and 1815'.

Napoleon set himself the task of creating a Third Germany to balance and counteract the newly achieved power of Prussia and the old-established prestige of the Habsburg monarchy. Prussia had withdrawn from the coalition against France in 1795, even before the start of Napoleon's meteoric rise, but his successive defeats of Austria and her allies during the next ten years allowed him, first of all to annex to France all of the German lands on the west bank of the Rhine and turn them into departments of that republic (soon to become an Empire) one and indivisible, and also to force upon the Holy Roman Emperor a thorough-going simplification of the map of Germany by the decrees (of 1803) extinguishing all the ecclesiastical states, and most of the free cities and petty sovereignties of the imperial knights east of that river. These lands were added to the territories of the larger German states—Prussia, Württemburg, Bavaria, Baden,

[1] See pp. 166–70.

Hessen and Nassau, as 'compensation' for their losses west of the Rhine, while those German rulers who had been readiest to do Napoleon's bidding were given even greater rewards, the Dukes of Württemburg and Bavaria, for instance, being given the titles of king. But theirs was, in reality, a state of vassalage, and in 1806 they were forced, at his command, to secede from the Holy Roman Empire and to join a Confederation of the Rhine, the constitution of which he had fabricated, and which completed the Third Germany that was to separate Prussia from Austria and keep them both in check in the interests of France and her emperor.

Faced by a characteristic Napoleonic ultimatum, fifteen middle German states immediately entered the Confederation of the Rhine. Subsequently others were 'permitted' to join it, so that it extended into north Germany and even to the Elbe, the Oder and the Vistula in the years after 1806. Napoleon was named as 'Protector' of the Confederation and each member state had to contribute levies to any war in which France or the Confederation was involved. A sham legislature or Diet was established and a 'fundamental statute' was promised, though the latter never was drawn up. Napoleon thus completed the process he had started at Lunéville in 1801 of reducing Germany to impotence. His victories in 1806 at Austerlitz against Austria, at the head of yet another coalition, and at Jena against a Prussia at last shamed out of her ten years' neutrality, strengthened his hand even more, for Saxony, Oldenburg and Mecklenburg were forced into the Confederation (in 1807) and the kingdom of Westphalia (presided over by his brother Jerome) and the Grand Duchy of Warsaw were added to it (in 1807 and in 1809 respectively) after Prussia had been crushed and had lost more than half her territory and after Napoleon's agreement with the Tsar Alexander I had settled the fate of Prussian Poland. The Confederation of the Rhine was now in fact the dominating political factor in Germany, for Prussia was reduced to the status of a petty principality and the Habsburg monarchy had been bereft of almost all its German-speaking territories and was now mainly inhabited by Slavs, Magyars and Italians.

Though it did not last, Napoleonic Germany was a masterly concept. Devised in the interests of France and her emperor, it nevertheless marked an important step forwards in the political evolution of the Germans themselves. 'The political map of Germany was simplified and more was done for the cause of good government in the valleys of the Danube, the Neckar and the Main than had been effected by all the policies of the eighteenth century' writes H. A. L. Fisher, and this is by no means an over-statement. Much of Napoleon's work in Germany was undone at Vienna, but there was much that nothing could undo. After Napoleon had finished with her, Germany may not already have been a nation, but she had become much more than a geographical expression.[1]

---

[1] The author's *Modern Constitutions since 1787* (Macmillan, 1939) describes (in chapter IV) the institutions of Napoleonic Germany in more detail than there was space for here.

CHAPTER VIII

THE CONSOLIDATION AND PARTITION OF PRUSSIA

THE rise of Prussia was the 'success-story' of the eighteenth century. Sweden and the Netherlands declined to the status of minor powers; France and the Habsburg monarchy, top-heavy with institutional decay, barely maintained their position as great powers, and then only by burying the hatchet of their age-old rivalry in the diplomatic revolution of 1756; Russia was still only half Europeanized, despite the efforts of Peter and Catherine; Britain, victor over France in three great wars and the heir to the latter's overseas Empire, herself passed under a cloud when her North American seaboard colonies successfully rebelled against her as the last quarter of the century dawned; Spain sank further and further into the background; the states of Italy and the lesser states of Germany were all on too small a scale to make their weight felt; only Prussia went through the century from strength to strength almost to its end.

This phenomenal advance was due in no small measure to a remarkable sequence of rulers of the Hohenzollern dynasty (Electors of Brandenburg from early in the fifteenth century, and of Brandenburg-Prussia from 1618 to 1701, when they became Kings in Prussia) beginning with the Elector Frederick William in 1640 and continuing with the Elector Frederick III (afterwards King Frederick I), and with King Frederick

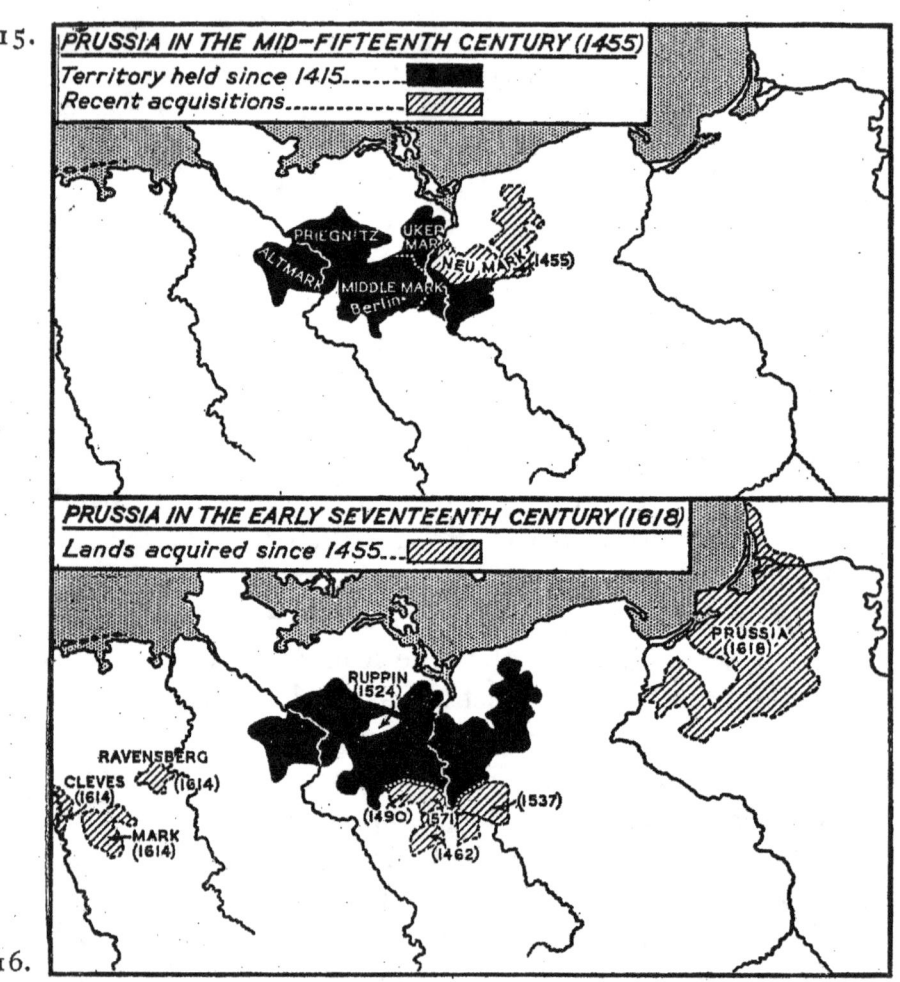

MAPS 15-18. THE EXPANSION OF

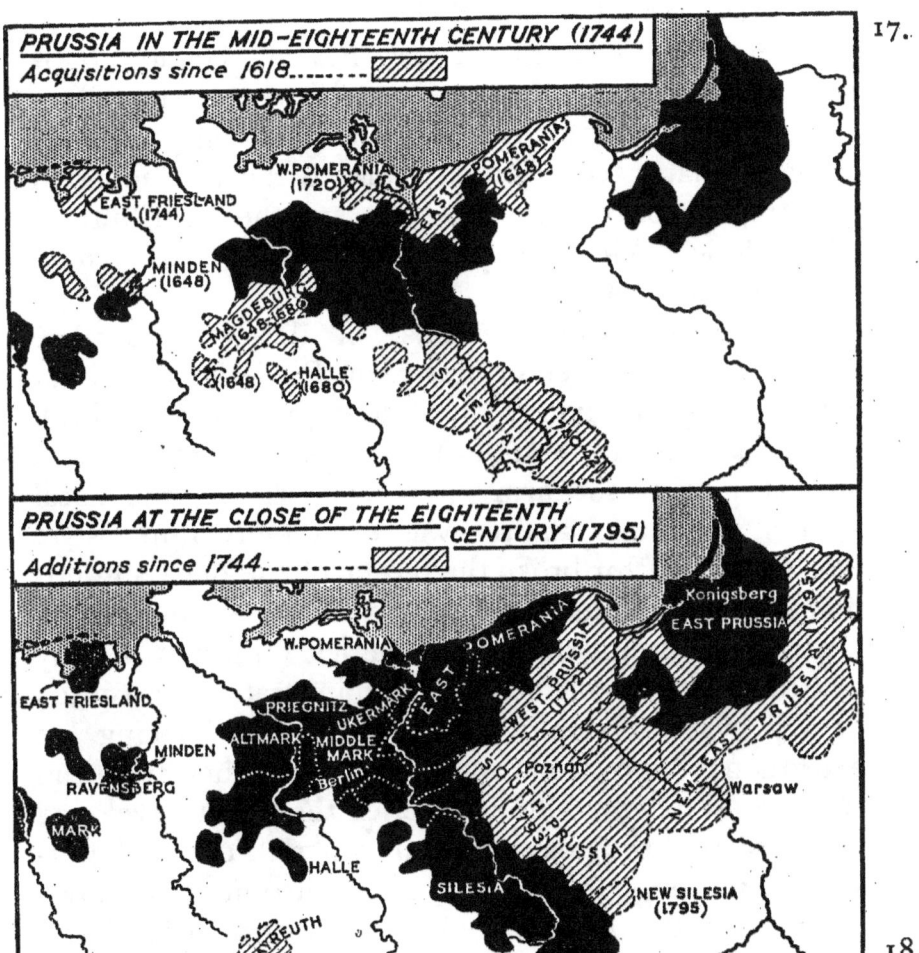

BRANDENBURG-PRUSSIA, 1415-1795

William I and King Frederick II, and only ending with the latter's death in 1786. Of these four men, whose reigns spanned a full century and a half all but four years, two earned during their lifetimes, and have been confirmed by posterity in the title of 'Great'. It is difficult to say whether the Great Elector (1640–88) or Frederick the Great (1740–86), who thus reigned exactly a century later, contributed more to the consolidation and progress of the Prussian state, and the contributions of Frederick William I and of Frederick I were only slightly less remarkable.

The territorial acquisitions[1] of these rulers were spectacular (by the end of his reign Frederick the Great ruled over $5\frac{1}{2}$ million people and 76,000 square miles), but their reorganization of the machinery of government and of policy—the army, the civil service, the fiscal system, economic affairs—was even more impressive. The Great Elector broke the power of the once autonomous local estates and magnates and founded a centralized administration. Frederick William I, a truly dedicated ruler, polished this administration to a pitch of efficiency, discipline and obedience (making no exception of his own son and heir) that no other European state could match, while Frederick the Great developed and exploited the possibilities of this well-oiled administrative machine, full treasury and well-trained spit-and-polish army that he inherited, until the once insignificant state of Brandenburg-Prussia was able to challenge the long-unquestioned paramountcy of the Habsburgs in Germany and to drive them from fear of it into the arms of their hereditary enemies, the kings of France, in 1756.

The state of which Frederick professed to be 'the

[1] See maps on pp. 116–17.

first servant' (whereas Louis XIV had claimed 'I am the state') was beginning the run down hill even before his death in 1786, so great had been the strains to which his wars had subjected it, but those wars (and his work during the short interludes of peace that he vouchsafed himself—and Europe) had not only sprawled the name of Prussia right across the map of Europe from west of the Rhine to east of the Niemen, but had raised her to the status of a power of the first magnitude. Her subsequent period of eclipse between 1795 and 1806 did not see undone all the work that Frederick the Great and his three predecessors had done, and a country and a people of a fibre less tough could not have recovered all the lost ground, and more, so rapidly during the era of liberation. After the liberation Prussia still had to take second place to Austria among the powers of Germany—but not for long. Her hegemony over Germany and her control over the balance of power in Europe during the Bismarckian age was based firmly (as Bismarck himself acknowledged) upon foundations laid in the eighteenth century.

CHAPTER IX

THE HABSBURG EMPIRE AS A 'GERMAN' POWER

LIKE the two arms of a giant see-saw Austria gradually sank down while Prussia rose up through the eighteenth century. Frederick the Great's League of Princes against the Emperor Joseph II in 1785 produced a state of transient equilibrium, but the *sans culottes* of the French Revolution and the lieutenant of artillery from Corsica were soon to sit so firmly on the fulcrum that the Habsburg-Hohenzollern rivalry could not be resumed in its full intensity until Napoleon's defeat in 1814 permitted such luxuries to return. Although the skill of Prince Metternich was to give (and for some thirty years more to maintain) the advantage to Austria, the settlement of 1814–15 made it impossible for her to recover permanently the paramount and unchallenged position she had possessed before Frederick the Great had repudiated the Pragmatic Sanction in 1740, and a non-Habsburg (the Elector of Bavaria) had been briefly placed on the shadowy throne of the Holy Roman Empire. The Empire, ever since 1648 an almost useless appendage to the many other Habsburg titles, was finally to disappear in 1806, but before that date the seeds of decay had been sown broadcast through the wide-flung Habsburg realms, and the 'reforms' of Maria Theresa (1740–80) and of her son Joseph II (1780–90)[1] came far

[1] Joseph II was Holy Roman Emperor and Emperor of Austria from 1780 to his death in 1790.

too late to arrest the growth of the choking weeds that were to enmesh and sap the vitality of the Habsburg state in the nineteenth century. While Prussia polished and sharpened her power to a razor-edge of efficiency under Frederick the Great and his three predecessors, a succession of mediocrities, both royal and ministerial, bedevilled the Habsburg realm. The French alliance of 1756 was a counsel of panic, seeking to bolster up by an unpopular foreign alliance a state of affairs at home that was already getting out of hand. Wise after their fashion, and to the extent of their somewhat limited vision, Maria Theresa and Joseph next resorted to internal reforms, but so heterogeneous was their realm that nothing could satisfy all parts of it at once. The Germans hated (and were hated by) the Poles, the Bohemians, the Magyars, the Slovenians and the other peoples of the monarchy, who all disliked each other; the Catholic Church resented toleration and secularization; the magnates objected to any attempt at emancipating the peasants and assuaging their land-hunger; the bourgeoisie was suspicious of all schemes of rural reform, while the countryside resented any advance, under imperial or royal patronage, in the status or the economic privileges of the towns. It was a vicious circle out of which no political genius could perhaps have brought the Habsburg monarchy at any time after the middle of the seventeenth century. Thus Austria's extremity was Prussia's opportunity, and the efficiency and comparative simplicity of the Prussian state-machine, as it had evolved by the middle of the eighteenth century, stood in strong contrast to the decrepit, top-heavy, Habsburg administration, pulled all ways at once by conflicting interests—ethnic, religious, economic, social and political.

The most serious defect of the Habsburg position in

Germany in the eyes, not only of Prussians, but of the inhabitants of all the other German states as well, was that by the eighteenth century they no longer ruled over a 'German' state at all. The German-speaking population constituted only a minority in the Empire of Austria, while in the kingdom of Hungary, where the Habsburgs also ruled, an overwhelming majority of the people was of non-German stock. Joseph II was conscious of this when he attempted to give up the Austrian Netherlands, an outlying and alien part of his dominions, in exchange for Bavaria, lying in the very heart of Germany and German through and through, but both his mother (and predecessor) the Empress Maria Theresa and his brother (and successor) the Emperor Leopold II, increased the non-German content of their inheritance by participating in the three Partitions of Poland (1775, 1792 and 1795), in the first of which he, too, as heir-apparent and co-ruler, had acquiesced.

Mirabeau somewhat maliciously described the Prussian state after the death of Frederick the Great as 'rotten before it is ripe'. By the time of Joseph II's death the Habsburg monarchy was rotten from over-ripeness.

CHAPTER X

THE LESSER STATES OF GERMANY

THE well-drilled Prussia bequeathed by his philistine father to Frederick the Great to serve as the instrument of his power-politics was hardly a *Kultur-Staat*. Frederick, who preferred to speak and write in French, had only the lowest opinion of the cultural possibilities of his country or of his subjects; and indeed their achievements in this sphere up to and during his lifetime were not very considerable. Prussia in the eighteenth century produced a few great men (such as Kant and Herder, both natives of East Prussia), but they were the exceptions that proved the rule. When the need for new ideas became urgent after the humiliations of the decade which ended with Jena and Tilsit, it was to natives of other German states, such as the Freiherr von Stein, that Prussia had to turn to put her house in order.

Although the court of the Habsburgs at Vienna was a much more important cultural centre than the bleak 'garrison-capital' of Berlin during the eighteenth century, original thinking and creative endeavour tended even there to be stifled by a fiercely strict etiquette and a conservatism of outlook that was only too natural in an administration which no longer felt so sure of itself as in the past, and prayed for the return of a golden age. Austria, indeed, resisted the forces of the *Aufklärung* with great tenacity, and her 'enlightened' rulers Maria Theresa and Joseph II were more unpopular at home *because* they were enlightened than for perhaps any other reason.

The enlightenment[1] indeed came to Germany mainly by and through the lesser states and the free cities. Its greatest product and its heir, Wolfgang von Goethe (1749–1832), was a native of the imperial city of Frankfurt-am-Main and took as his patron the Duke of Saxe-Weimar-Eisenach, to whom he became chief political as well as cultural adviser. Württemburg, Bavaria, Hanover, Hessen, Saxony and a number of other lesser states, though the *Aufklärung* burned less brightly in some of them than in others, all outshone both the Habsburg and the Hohenzollern realms in their receptivity to its influence. Much scorn has been poured on the German *Kleinstaat* of the eighteenth century, with its aping of Versailles, its petty intrigues, its ostentatious and often bankrupt rulers, in peace-time a prey to the whims of favourites and of mistresses, and weather-vanes towards the highest bidder in war, but, in some cases at least, it did experiment with new ideas and theories of government, did accept stimulus from the outside world, and did subsidize learning and the arts for their own sakes and not merely for their prestige-and-power-bringing possibilities.

Württemberg, in particular, had a most singular history in the eighteenth century, which ran counter to the general trend of what may be called naked absolutism slowly broadening down to enlightened despotism. In Württemberg, the power of the estates or Diet, first established in the fifteenth century, and based firmly upon the sixteenth-century Pact of Tübingen, was sufficient to withstand the efforts of the Duke Charles Eugene (1737–93) to raise taxes without its consent and to

[1] See further pp. 159–165.

legislate without reference to it. He was made to reconfirm the Pact of Tübingen and surrender his absolutist pretensions. Even before the influence of the American and French Revolutions came to be felt in Germany, therefore, the state of Württemberg had a parliament of a modern type. The 'advanced' constitution of 1819, thus, when it was offered to Württemberg by its king (as its duke had become in 1806 under Napoleon's protection), came not as a great innovation, breaking completely with the past, but as yet another stage in a political evolution which had long-since outstripped that of all the larger German states and all but very few of the petty states and territories. The political retrogression which almost all the other 'liberalized' states of Germany suffered during some part or other of the era of Metternich, was hardly experienced at all by Württemberg. The constitution of 1819 proved so durable indeed that, although it was by this time somewhat out of date, it was put into operation again in 1850 and remained in existence until the kingdom of Württemberg itself ceased to be in the Revolution of 1918, and was succeeded by a republic that was one of the federated *Länder* of Weimar Germany. This steady development of Württemberg, by contrast with the stormy fortunes of her neighbours Bavaria and Baden during the upheavals of the nineteenth century, was due in no small measure to the survival of the medieval estates until they could be replaced by a modern constitutional régime. The parallel with the constitutional evolution of Britain, despite many variations on points of detail, is obvious, and indeed is much more marked in Württemberg than in Hanover, despite the personal union of that state with Britain between 1714 and 1837.

Part IV   *Germany and the World*

CHAPTER I

GERMANY AND THE ROMAN EMPIRE

GERMANY, too, can be described as having been divided into three parts at the time of Julius Caesar. There was, first of all, that part west of the Rhine and south of the Danube which was completely incorporated within the Roman Empire, was colonized and was romanized; then there was that series of territories—between the Rhine and the Weser in the north, stretching some way up the Lahn and Main valleys in the centre, and across the Neckar and the upper and middle Danube (in what is now Bavaria and Austria) in the south—which were only briefly held and partially colonized, very much along the lines of a military occupation only; finally (and this was by far the larger part of what we now know as Germany) there was the extensive area inhabited by Germanic tribes to which Roman rule or occupation never extended. This last was the *Germania Magna* charted by Ptolemy and described equally impressionistically by Tacitus, and its inhabitants were the tribes which were to overrun the *limes* of the Roman Empire in the fifth century A.D. and to produce leaders who founded the Merovingian and Carolingian Empires, both of which Empires were to be dominated by the most enterprising of all these groups of Germanic tribes, the Franks. In the days of Julius Caesar and Augustus, of Trajan and of Marcus Aurelius, the Franks still lived well to the east of the Rhine and had little or no contact with Roman civilization. Arminius (or Hermann), who defeated Varus and destroyed his army in the *Teutoburgerwald* in A.D. 9 when Roman power was attempting to expand to beyond the river Weser, was not a Frank, but a chieftain of the Cherusci, a branch of the Saxons, who were later to be conquered by the Franks.

Julius Caesar established the line of the river Rhine from its mouth almost to its source as the limit of his conquests eastwards from Gaul, and his expedition east of that river in 55 B.C. across a bridge he built near the Lorelei rock at St. Goar, was only a brief reconnaissance, like his invasion of Britain in the same year. Although he seems to have contemplated securing the line of the Danube also, he in fact left this task to his successor Augustus, who established the new provinces of Rhaetia (covering approximately south-eastern Switzerland, Western Austria and southern Bavaria of today), of Noricum (Styria) in 15 B.C. and of Pannonia (eastern Austria and western Hungary) in A.D. 10, when the last of these was separated from Dalmatia. The line of the lower Danube was also secured by the creation of the province of Moesia (approximately covering the areas of Serbia and Bulgaria as they were from 1878 to 1918) in A.D. 6, and settling many thousands of landless and wandering Dacians from across the Danube in the new province.

Augustus and his generals were indeed much more successful in occupying and colonizing the extreme southern or sub-alpine strip of Germany up to the Danube than they were in extending Roman control east of the Rhine into *Germania Magna* north of the Main and in the direction of the Elbe. This latter policy went from frustration to frustration, not unmixed with disaster (as in A.D. 9) and finally his successor Tiberius recalled his general Germanicus in A.D. 16 to the Rhine frontier once and for all. Here two military zones, *Germania Superior* and *Germania Inferior*, were formed immediately west of the river, joining at a point between Bonn and Coblenz. The limits of *Germania Superior* extended eastwards with the river beyond its great bend at Basel, following it as far as Lake Constance, and then ran back through Lake Zurich and Lake Lucerne to Lake Geneva, keeping north of the line of the high Alps. *Germania Inferior* and *Germania Superior* were, it must be remembered, inhabited at this time (unlike *Germania Magna*) mainly by Celtic tribes (the Germanic peoples having only broken across the Rhine briefly and in small numbers), and their civilization, as part of the Roman Empire, was Romano-Celtic. Augustus and his leaders, in their ambition to establish an Elbe frontier (and the land between lower Rhine and lower Elbe was loosely occupied and perfunctorily colonized for some twenty years before the Varus disaster), probably had in mind the defence in depth of Italy and Gaul against the Germanic invader—and the conquest of Rhaetia, Noricum and Pannonia, was an obvious concomitant to this. The success of their plan might have altered the whole future course of European history. After their time the internal dissensions of the Empire and the increased pressure of fresh and more powerful Germanic tribes made it impossible to revive this policy. Perhaps *Germania Magna* (the 'Great' or classic Germany of subsequent history, and the core of the Holy Roman Empire) came nearest to being incorporated completely within the Roman system in the years between 12 B.C. and 6 B.C., when Drusus undertook his great 'combined operation' by land and sea to and up the Elbe valley, and Ahenobarbus pushed northwards across the Danube, up the Naab and down the Saale river where it runs into the middle Elbe. The campaigns of Tiberius at this time, in the region bounded by the rivers mentioned and by the Rhine, and his transfer from *Germania Magna* of many Germans into settlements in Gaul, where they could be more easily supervised and romanized, represents the high-water mark of this short-lived enveloping movement. Never again was a serious and comprehensive attempt to be made by Rome to reduce and colonize *Germania Magna*. All that was done, later in the first century A.D. (in the reigns of Vespasian and Domitian), was to occupy and partially to colonize the area within the great bend of the Rhine pivoting on Basel where *Germania Magna* thrust a dangerous salient south and westwards, pointing directly at the heart of Gaul. This area, named *Agri Decumates* by the Romans (and occupying approximately the area of the modern German state of Baden and parts of Hessen and Württemberg) was never given the status of a province, although later it was to be added to Vindelicia (the northern part of Rhaetia) for administrative purposes. From the first to the third centuries this area was held, and very heavily fortified along its eastern boundaries by successive emperors, by the defensive wall and ditch known as the *limes*, stretching southwards from the river Lahn near its mouth, through the Taunus hills, along the river Main for a short distance (near Aschaffenburg) down the hills paralleling the river Neckar in its middle course (from about Heilbronn to Esslingen) and somewhat to the east of it, and finally turning eastwards across country to reach the Danube near Regensburg, there to connect up with that other great line of defences on the north side of that river stretching, eventually, to the Black Sea. This great south-west German counter-salient, established definitely in A.D. 83, was to be overrun by the Alemanni in the fourth century and almost completely de-romanized during the Dark Ages, but it nevertheless remains to this day 'a borderland between Romance and German civilizations', and the great modern spa of Baden-Baden, which was used as a watering place by the Romans, was to become a cosmopolitan centre again in the nineteenth and twentieth centuries, and, ironically enough, as the capital of the French Zone of Occupation after 1945, a new spearhead of Romance penetration in the *Germania* of our own day.

Throughout the second century the Rhine frontier of the Roman Empire (unlike that of the Danube) was comparatively quiet. Hadrian strengthened the *limes* and the Antonines straightened them and strengthened them still further east of the Neckar river, but Trajan was not called upon to defend the frontiers here in the vigorous way he had to in Dacia, north of the lower Danube (in campaigns celebrated by the carvings on his famous column, which still stands in Rome). Although the Alemanni and the Franks broke into Gaul before the end of the third century, they were thrown back by Probus in A.D. 280 and did not bother Diocletian during the twenty years of his remarkable reign (284–305). Little did it seem, in the year A.D. 330, when Constantine removed himself from Rome to a second capital on the Bosphorus, that within a hundred years the frontiers of the Rhine, the *limes* and the Danube, which had stood for upwards of four centuries, would no longer exist.

By the year 476 the whole of the Rhine valley was overrun by the powerful Germanic tribes of the Franks and the Alemanni, while the Friesians occupied the marshlands and islands near that river's mouth. Gaul and the Iberian peninsula had both also been almost completely occupied by Germanic tribes. Beyond the Franks and the Alemanni to the eastward, other tribes such as the Saxons, the Thuringians and the Marcomanni (later to be known as the Bavarians) were attempting to press into what had for so long been Roman Europe. The Empire was in ruins and its urban civilization had all but disappeared north of the Alps, but the fact that it had held on to these lands west of the Rhine and south of the Danube for so many centuries, left an indelible stamp upon western and central Europe on both sides of those rivers that has never been obliterated during a millenium and a half of subsequent history. Rome may never have conquered Germany, but she converted the Germans into west Europeans by her prestige and her example, and went on doing so when her Empire no longer existed.

CHAPTER II

THE CAROLINGIAN EXPERIMENT

THE tribal group which dominated western and central Europe from the fifth to the ninth century A.D. was that of the Franks. They founded two great dynasties, the Merovingian and the Carolingian, and the dominions of their rulers at their greatest extent stretched from Barcelona on the Mediterranean to Schleswig on the shores of the Baltic, from Rennes in Brittany to Tulln on the Danube (near Vienna), to the peninsula of Istria on the Adriatic, and in Italy almost to Monte Cassino.

The Franks had hammered at the gates of the Roman Empire without avail during the third (when they first appeared there) and the fourth centuries of the Christian era—the Emperor Julian settled the defeated Salian Franks in Brabant and around Antwerp in A.D. 358—but by the middle of the fifth century they had broken down the northern *limes* and had found their way across the Rhine into the valleys of the Moselle, the Meuse and the Scheldt. At the same time, from their capital at 'Frankfort' they were able to push back the Thuringians to the east of them and occupy the whole of the Main valley, east of the Rhine, as well. This was the Empire that their first great leader, Clovis, under whom they were converted to Catholic Christianity, inherited in A.D. 481. He extended it by conquering the land of the Alemanni (or Suebi) of the upper Danube and middle Rhine valleys and also the lands of the romanized Celts

MAP 19. THE KINGDOM OF THE FRANKS
From *Der Grosse Herder*

comprising almost all the Seine and Loire basins in what is now France, and beyond them as far as the river Garonne, before his death in A.D. 511. A century later (in 618) the Frankish Empire included virtually the whole of the area of modern France and Switzerland and still continued to dominate the basin of the Rhine and its tributaries, though its eastward movement had now

THE CAROLINGIAN EXPERIMENT

virtually stopped. The rest of the seventh century was one of confusion, when the Merovingian dynasty became effete and Mayors of the Palace ruled the great subdivisions of the Frankish Empire—Austrasia, Neustria, Burgundy and Aquitaine—as if they were sovereign princes. A century later (in A.D. 714) one of these, Charles Martel of Neustria, founded the Carolingian dynasty named after him and reunited the Frankish lands under his strong rule. He also stopped the Arab advance into Europe at Poitiers in A.D. 732. He and his successor, Pepin III, added few territories to the Empire between 714 and 768, and on the death of the latter it was briefly divided between his two sons. The survivor of these, Charles the Great, who ruled from 768 to 814, resumed the drive of Frankish power to the east and to the south, and shortly before his death had brought the Carolingian Empire to its widest extent by conquering the Saxons, annexing the kingdom of Lombardy (comprising the northern half of Italy) and occupying the Spanish march beyond the Pyrenees. Even beyond these definitive frontiers of his realm he defeated Avars on the middle Danube, dominated the lands of the Wends and the Sorbs between the Elbe and the Oder and temporarily occupied the north bank of the Ebro river in Spain. With the exception of the major part of the Iberian peninsula, he controlled an area as extensive as—and in the north-east more extensive than—the west Roman Empire when it had been divided from the eastern.

It therefore seemed only logical that he should accept the crown and the title of a Roman emperor in the year A.D. 800 in the capital of the old Empire, at the hands of the Pope he had liberated and protected. This act did not make him the heir to Rome except in his own eyes and those of his immediate followers and councillors,

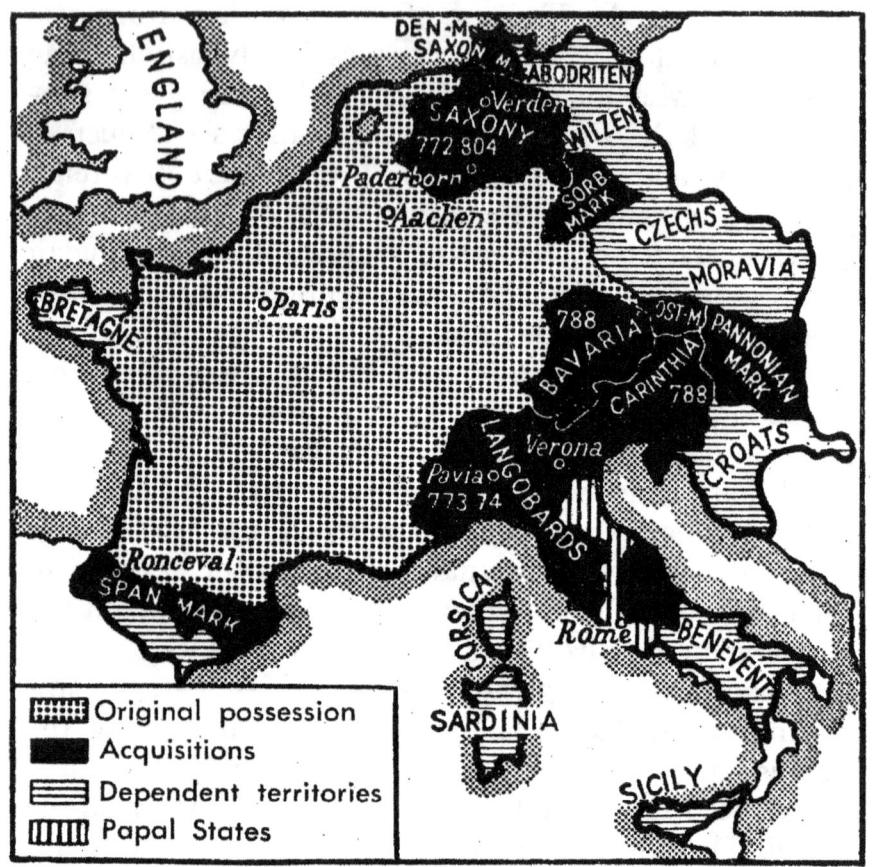

MAP 20. THE EMPIRE OF CHARLES THE GREAT
From *Der Grosse Herder*

and throughout his life the East Roman emperors in Byzantium continued to ignore his new status and his self-assumed and grandiloquent title of *Augustus a Deo coronatus magnus pacificus imperator Romanum gubernans imperium*.

Charles the Great, in fact, wielded his great power and influence in the Europe of his day because he was King of the Franks and ruler over the Frankish Empire. His Roman title may have given him some satisfaction and the

Papacy much more, but it did not materially increase his prestige. After his death it meant even less to his sole heir Louis the Pious, and the Frankish monarchy was partitioned in A.D. 843, the Carolingian dynasty finally coming to an end in 887. Charlemagne's Empire was of a very short-term nature and his crowning in Rome in 800 would have possessed much less significance in European or in world history had not a later 'Holy Roman Empire' sought to establish a continuity, which in fact never existed, with the Empire of Charlemagne.

It has already been stated that Charlemagne was neither a French nor a German king, for the Carolingian Empire antedated any clear-cut differentiation between what came to be known only after the partition of Verdun of A.D. 843 as 'Germany' and 'France'. The first real king of Germany was Henry the Fowler (in A.D. 918) and the first real king of France was Hugh Capet (in 987). It may likewise be claimed that Charlemagne was never a Roman emperor in any real sense of the term. His main interests always lay north of the Alps, and he probably himself never attached any very great importance to the crowning of the year 800. Certainly he never exploited it to any significant extent. His wide-flung Empire, his establishment of marches against the Muslims and the Slavs, his defences against the Northmen, his extension of Catholic Christianity to the remotest parts of his realm, his patronage of learning, the peace and order he imposed upon such a large section of Europe—the most extensive peace since that of Rome had disintegrated four hundred years earlier—all these had great significance. Without the Carolingian Empire Germany and France as the modern world knows them might never have evolved as they did, or developed in wealth and civilization so rapidly in the 'high Middle Ages' which

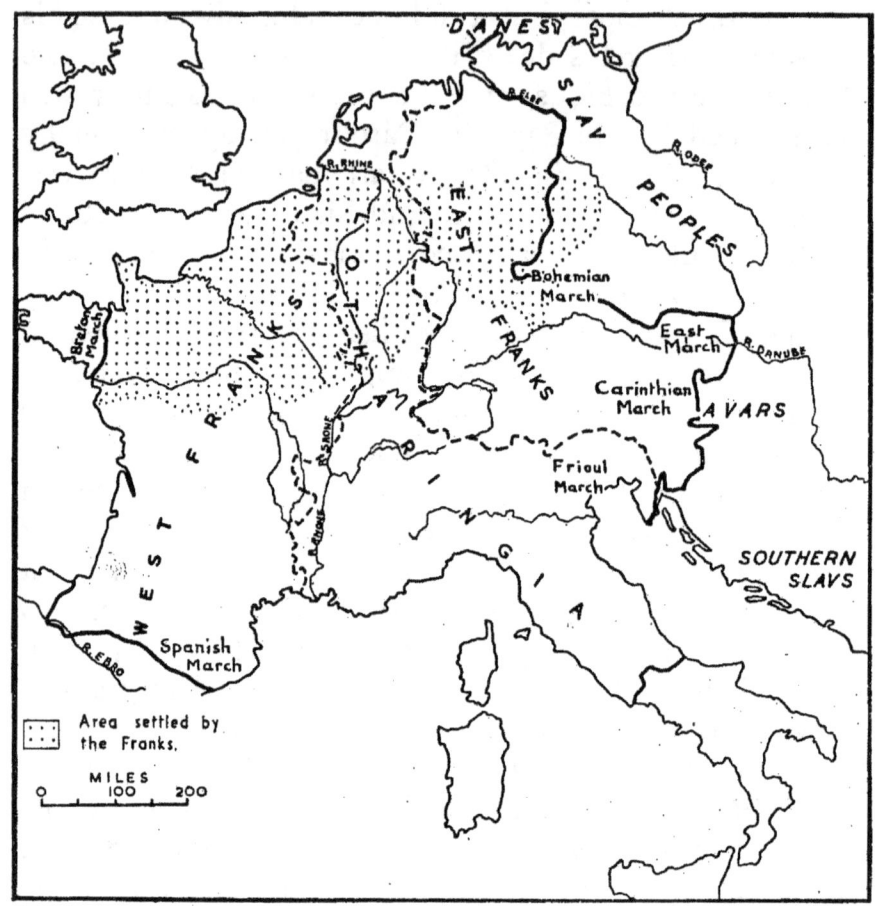

MAP 21. THE PARTITION OF VERDUN, A.D. 843
—*after Hoffman*

came long after the days of Charlemagne. That makes of Charlemagne and his Empire the precursors of many things, but it does not make them responsible for such developments as the great struggle between Empire and Papacy which broke out so much later and so bedevilled German history, nor for the chronic disunion into which Germany was to fall in the later Middle Ages. These had other and different roots.

CHAPTER III

THE HOLY ROMAN EMPIRE: MYTH AND REALITY

CHARLEMAGNE did not create the Holy Roman Empire any more than he created 'Germany'. Under their long subjection to the Frankish monarchy the various Germanic peoples acquired so much feeling of belonging together that, after the partitions which ended the Carolingian Empire, they accepted a common king, elected by and from among the various rulers of their tribal duchies. Henry the Fowler and the first two Ottos created and consolidated the German monarchy only in the tenth century, and the term *regnum teutonicum* is first known to have been used in A.D. 920, more than a century after the death of Charles the Great.

The true creator of the medieval Empire was indeed Otto I, whose crowning in Rome in the year 967 is its true beginning, rather than the event of the year 800. After 967 the Saxon and Salian emperors were for a century truly emperors of the West (Otto II was the first of them to call himself *Roman* Emperor), acknowledged as such both in Rome and in Constantinople, and controlling the north half of Italy as well as Germany. They gave that protection to the Pope of which the destruction of the Carolingian Empire had deprived him, and up to the end of the reign of the Emperor Henry III the Papacy was, in effect, controlled and dominated by the Emperor. For over a century, therefore, from 967 to

1076, when Henry IV came into conflict with a reformed Papacy, there was no real rivalry between the lay and the ecclesiastical leaders of the West. The Emperor ruled Germany with the close collaboration of the German bishops, and he controlled the largest part of Italy with the support and connivance of the Pope, who nevertheless was accorded a special position as a temporal ruler in his immediate dominions, like any other prince or duke. There was no question of equality between the two, any more than either Pepin or Charles the Great or Otto I had regarded the Pope as his equal when he was gracious enough to permit the bishop of Rome to crown him and claim his protection.

The full title of Holy Roman Emperor was only claimed in 1254 after the death of Frederick II, and on the eve of the great interregnum—though the term Roman Emperor was regularly used in the West from 1034 and the title 'King of the Romans' for the emperor-elect from 1040. Only a century after this, in 1157, was the term *Holy* Empire in common use—so the evolution of the title was a slow one. It remained for the Emperor Maximilian I at the end of the fifteenth century to coin the title 'Holy Roman Empire of the German Nation' and to abandon the pretence that the Habsburgs had inherited the title or the prestige of the West Roman Emperors. This was in the first age of modern German Nationalism, an age which invented the Barbarossa myth, but was incapable of understanding the motives that had prompted Charlemagne and the Ottos to let themselves be crowned in Rome. Farther away in time from Charlemagne and the Ottos than these rulers had been from the last true Roman emperors of the west, they took their ideas of the emperor from theories invented or crystallized in the thirteenth and fourteenth centuries. After the year 1250 only five emperors were actually crowned by the Pope, and no Habsburg emperor other than the tradition-ridden Charles V was among them. Even he was not crowned in Rome.

The fact was that the imperial title was an incubus rather than a help to those who bore it after 1250, and the Habsburgs dominated Germany during the later history of the Holy Roman Empire because of their great territorial possessions and their successful marriage alliances rather than through having secured a 'corner' in the imperial title, as they did in the fourteenth century after the Luxemburg dynasty had come to an end. After A.D. 1250 the Empire had virtually no crown-lands left in Germany, the electoral principle had been so firmly established that the emperor was little more than a puppet of the princes, making so many concessions to secure his election that his title was an empty one as soon as he assumed it. The princes made this abundantly clear when they forced the Luxemburg Emperor Charles IV to issue the Golden Bull in A.D. 1356. Not until the reign of Maximilian I at the end of the fifteenth century was the decentralization imposed upon Germany since the twelfth century (and underlined so clearly in the Golden Bull) challenged—and the challenge made by Maximilian and his successor Charles V was to be unsuccessful. A century after the end of Charles V's reign an even more disastrous and logically complete decentralization was to be accepted for Germany by the emperor's acceptance of the terms of the Treaty of Westphalia. Even before that date the emperor had been a cypher. After it he became an anomaly.

Yet the imperial title dragged on its well-nigh useless existence until the beginning of the nineteenth century, but even in mid-eighteenth century it was considered by the Habsburgs to be sufficiently valuable for them to make extensive treaty concessions in order to retain it for their heirs (the Pragmatic Sanction of 1740), to fight wars for (the War of the Austrian Succession) and to make peace and an alliance with their age-long enemies the Bourbons for (the Diplomatic Revolution of 1756). Even the Emperor Francis might not have renounced the title in 1806 if Napoleon had not first made a laughing-stock and a mockery of it by creating the Confederation of the Rhine and forcing most of the electors to secede from something that was in no geographical, traditional or any other sense Roman, by no stretch of the imagination (especially since the secularizing age of Joseph II) Holy, and was an Empire only in name.

CHAPTER IV

GERMANY AND THE MEDIEVAL PAPACY

A VERY remarkable man, one of the most powerful figures of the whole Middle Ages, brought to a head the conflict between the Papacy and the emperors which so bedevilled the remainder of medieval history—and the history of Germany far into the modern period. The man was Hildebrand, who became Pope as Gregory VII in the year 1073. This alumnus of Cluny, a man of iron resolution and of fanatical devotion to the policy he considered essential for the Papacy and for western Christendom, completely wrecked during the twelve short years of his pontificate the possibility either of a peaceful partnership between Papacy and Empire or of further normal development in the direction of unity and strong government for Germany, comparable to that which was to occur (with but minor deviations) in England under the Normans and Angevins and in France under the Capetians. This man Hildebrand, from the highest motives, did as much harm to Germany as did Adolf Hitler, from the basest of motives, in a comparable period of twelve years (1933-45) nearly nine centuries later. Different as these two men were in almost every possible way, they had this in common: both reached for the moon; both failed; but in their failure they destroyed much beside themselves.

The prohibition of the practices of simony (the sale of ecclesiastical offices) and of lay investiture, and the attempt to enforce this prohibition, as also that of the marriage of the clergy, were only the beginnings of Gregory VII's reforming zeal. His aim was to set up a theocracy in Christendom, with all lay rulers, including the Emperor, in the position of vassals to the Church and to the Papacy. A proud and active ruler such as Henry IV, whose state was, after his majority, the best organized in Europe, could not accept the position of subordination that the Pope, bolstering his theoretical extremism with historical claims that were palpably untenable, offered him in this 'new order'. Henry's surrender to Gregory at Canossa in A.D. 1077 did not indicate any change of heart, but was purely a strategic and a temporary retreat forced upon him by the rebellion of the German lay nobility while he was embroiled in Italy with the Pope—a Pope who, like his twelfth-century successor Innocent III, was not above inciting the Emperor's vassals to rebellion against him. Once the situation was in hand in Germany once more, Henry IV again defied the Pope and was again excommunicated, but this time he marched on Rome, captured the eternal city and drove Gregory VII to death in exile. The second round in this implacable struggle thus went to the Emperor, but, at the same time, the stature of his office had been reduced. No longer was he the Pope-maker, the protector of the spiritual head of Christendom; he was instead the champion of the lay power against the ecclesiastical, in a rivalry which was to become more bitter and legalistic as time went on. The 'compromise' solution to the problem of lay investiture propounded at the Diet of Worms by Henry V in 1122, provided the basis for a papal-imperial truce that lasted uneasily through the twelfth century—but even during that period Frederick Barbarossa refused to make feudal obeisance before Pope Adrian IV in 1155, and was on bad terms with Alexander III for many years until they patched up their quarrel in 1183.

Barbarossa's successor Henry VI (1190–97) carried the counter-attack upon the Papacy that Henry IV had begun and Barbarossa had re-started, to extreme lengths, and only his early death prevented the reduction of the Pope to the position of a mere bishop in Rome, with little authority beyond his immediate dominions and no control at all over Germany or the other territorial states north of the Alps. Henry's dominion over Sicily through his wife, and his agreements with the Lombard cities, produced an effective encirclement of papal territory. The ideals of Hildebrand seemed irrevocably lost.

But papal claims were to be revived by yet another protagonist, Innocent III, who was as ruthless and able, though hardly as fanatical, as Hildebrand himself had been. As tutor by remote-control to the young Frederick II (whose title as emperor was recognized at last in A.D. 1212), he did his best, but without avail, to instil into Frederick the idea of the papal being above the monarchical power, and after Innocent's death in 1216, Frederick, knowing that he had the Papacy encircled by his dominions even more effectively than had been the position under his father Henry VI, paid less and less attention to papal claims and went on his crusade in 1228 without the blessing of the Pope. Returning with the enhanced prestige of having secured possession of Jerusalem, the holy city, Frederick was even less inclined to listen to the claims and strictures of Gregory IX, and the lawyers, poets and pamphleteers who supported him became increasingly scurrilous in their references to the Pope—which the pro-papal controversialists repaid in good measure by stigmatizing the Emperor as the personification of antichrist.

In 1232, mindful no doubt of the success Gregory VII had achieved by instigating the German princes to rebel against Henry IV, Frederick II made very extensive concessions to his German vassals in his 'Constitution in favour of the Princes'—giving them virtual sovereignty in their respective dominions and fatally undermining the future authority of the emperors in Germany.

It has been truly said that in their fateful struggle from the days of Gregory VII and Henry IV onwards, 'both the Empire and the Papacy failed to recognize the mutual interdependence of *Imperium* and *Sacerdotium* . . . both powers overstressed their claims to absolute supremacy, and . . . both thereby not only undermined the foundations of their own political power but contributed to the dissolution of the supernational unity of western civilization' (Reinhardt). The Emperor sought to undermine the Pope's territorial position in Italy as assiduously as the Pope did the Emperor's in Germany —and both had succeeded only too well by the middle of the thirteenth century. Then, even more disastrously for the Empire and for Germany, the Papacy sought the alliance of other new and powerful territorial states that had arisen in western Europe, notably France and England. Before the end of the thirteenth century, after the anarchy of the interregnum that followed the death of Frederick II in 1250, the anomalous position had arisen that while the fate of Germany had fallen into the hands of the Papacy (which now had a vested interest in prolonging disunity and anarchy there), the Papacy itself had fallen virtually into the hands of France.

This state of affairs—leading to the 'Babylonish captivity' of the Popes at Avignon from A.D. 1309 to

1376—had resulted from the re-assertion of the papal claims in an extreme form by Boniface VIII in the course of his quarrel with Philip IV of France. The Bulls *Clericis Laicos* (1296) and *Unam Sanctam* (1302) represented the high-water mark of such claims, though John XXII, one of the Avignon Popes, was even to go farther in one respect and to assert his right to appoint the German King or Emperor. It was this preposterous claim that provoked the famous reply of Marsilius of Padua entitled *Defensor Pacis*, which went equally far against the Pope, and even denied the primacy of the bishops of Rome and appealed to the arbitrament of a General Council of the Church. This idea had great attractions to perplexed Christians in the days of the Great Schism (1378–1418) during which one Pope resided in Rome and a rival Pope in Avignon. The Council of Constance ended the Schism in 1418 (and for good measure burned at the stake the Bohemian heretic John Huss) and, by decreeing that a General Council had higher authority than the Pope, not only sided (in this respect) with Marsilius of Padua, but put an end to any hope of the successful revival of papal claims in the extreme form they had taken under Gregory VII, Innocent III and Boniface VIII. It was felt on all sides that a reform of the Papacy itself was now a much more pressing matter than increasing its powers over the secular arm.

Although the conciliar movement failed to reform the Papacy in the fifteenth century, and the authority of the Pope over a General Council was more or less successfully reasserted by Pius II in the Bull *Execrabilis* (1460), the Papacy was virtually as weak and lacking in authority in western Christendom by the middle of that century as was the Holy Roman Empire under the shadowy rule of

Frederick III. In their mutually weakened state, Papacy and Empire achieved the compromise peace of the Concordat of Vienna of 1448, which defined the respective spheres of influence of Church and state in Germany until the Lutheran revolt three-quarters of a century later threw everything once more into the melting-pot.

Much more than that of either England or of France (because of the connection with the Holy Roman Empire and also because of the claims and ambitions of successive Emperors in Italy) the history of Germany in the Middle Ages was thus bedevilled by this bitter four-century-long struggle of Empire and Papacy. From being the most advanced and united state in Europe under Henry III, Germany was to become one of the most disorganized and weak under Frederick III.

CHAPTER V

GERMANY AND THE REFORMATION

GERMANY's belated revenge for the continuous thwarting of her destinies by the Papacy from the eleventh century onwards was the Reformation. This, of course, does not mean that the Reformation, initiated at Wittenberg in Saxony by Martin Luther in 1517, was a conscious upsurge of German national feeling against papal interference. 'The German Nation' that Luther talked about in a famous pamphlet in 1521 was not yet so coherent an entity that it could react in any single direction at any one time about anything. Nevertheless, mixed with the malaise that existed among Christians everywhere, north and south of the Alps—Germans, Bohemians, Frenchmen, Italians, Englishmen, even Spaniards—by the beginning of the fifteenth century, on the subject of abuses in the Church and of the declining moral authority of the Papacy, there was a specially deep resentment among Germans, both lay and clerical, on account of the deep wounds that papal policy had left on the German body politic. In an age of consolidating nations and powerful centralizing rulers, like Ferdinand and Isabella in Spain and Louis XI in France, Germany (like Italy, though for rather different reasons) had no effective central government, no single foreign policy, no government-patronized expansion overseas, no feeling of pride in unity and united achievement. Wrongly or rightly many Germans identified this lack of political co-ordination and the feeling of frustration that resulted from it, with their social and religious malaise, and regarded the unreformed, unregenerate Papacy (which re-affirmed the Bull *Unam Sanctam* of Boniface VIII at the Fifth Lateran Council in 1517, the very year in which Luther produced his *Ninety-Five Theses*) as the cause of it all. Leadership in the struggle against papal pretensions had long since been abandoned by a helpless Empire, but it was not to be taken out of the hands of the Emperor by men arising from the midst of the German people, men of humble peasant origin such as Luther, of middle-class urban stock such as Melancthon, of the lesser and decayed nobility such as Ulrich von Hutton. It was these men, not the Emperor and his entourage, who were now to split Christianity, to administer to the Papacy its greatest defeat in history, and to put Germany back at the centre of the stage of European and world history. For nearly three centuries since the death of Frederick II she had waited in the wings, her heroic trappings of the *Kaiserzeit* gathering dust and going more and more out of fashion. It was not the slightly ludicrous Maximilian, called 'the last of the Knights', or the much more pompous and archaic-minded Charles V, who restored Germany's prestige among the nations in the sixteenth century, but an obscure young monk teaching theology at the University of Wittenberg, whose real ambitions were not of this world at all.

Martin Luther is an enigmatic figure. Time of course was on his side; had he been born in the days of Huss, he too would probably have gone to the stake. In France, in Britain, in Spain or in Italy at the beginning of the sixteenth century, he would not have found the opportunity and the platform with which Germany provided him. But, even allowing for all the advantages of the situation, in him the hour of decision found its man—a man of great intellectual vigour, of unwavering purpose and of unsurpassed dialectical skill. Added to this, his words had a popular and an earthy appeal which a great religious innovator requires, and which were needed in the sixteenth century (when the ordinary citizen was beginning to think for himself and consider what rights he possessed) as never before. It is no wonder that Luther's contribution to the literature and the language of Germany are considered as scarcely of less importance than his activities in the religious sphere. But Luther was not consciously contributing to literature; he wrote with a purpose and that purpose was spiritual regeneration—for himself, for the German people and for Christendom—perhaps in that order. He achieved all three.

The position of Martin Luther as a German patriot is an equivocal one, of course. He thought that Germany and the German Church were not receiving a fair deal from an alien Papacy, and he resented the sale of indulgences in part because it drew off good German wealth into the papal coffers in Rome, but he did not go to any extremes of chauvinism; he did not express anti-foreign sentiments; he did not, above all (though the National-Socialists have claimed him as a precursor), tell the Germans they were a master-race, destined to inherit the earth, or any similar nonsense. He gave them a new self-respect, and by 'breaking the bond of Rome' he turned a page in German history more decisively than perhaps any man until the days of Bismarck. But he did not consciously work for Germany's unity or better government, for the representation of the people (an idea which he would have abhorred) or for the absolutism of the Machiavellian type of Prince (a person to whom he would tend to have the very strongest moral objections). The long-term political consequences of his revolt were enormous, but his aims and immediate objectives were not political at all. This helps to explain some of his apparent inconsistencies of behaviour. To him the Peasants' War was not a popular rising to right deep-seated wrongs, but a violent mob outbreak against law and order. He sought the protection and patronage of absolute rulers such as Frederick the Wise of Saxony because they were prepared to further his religious aims, and his *Appeal to the Christian Nobility of the German Nation* saw him invoking the authority of an *élite* class in order to secure his ends. He was not seeking to further the interests of that *élite* class, though it was in fact to profit greatly by his activities and his exhortations.

The course of the Reformation in Germany and in Europe is an oft-told tale that need not be repeated here. That Germany was its breaking-out point and Martin Luther, a German monk, its central figure meant that Germany was to be more profoundly affected by the movement than any other land, but its effects elsewhere, as is well known, were also of fundamental importance. The religious frontiers drawn by the Reformation and re-drawn by the counter-Reformation split Germany into two confessional parts and then re-divided her once again, leaving her the prey to foreign latter-day 'crusaders', Protestant and Catholic alike, until the middle of the seventeenth century. This tragic situation cannot be laid at the door of Martin Luther, but was mainly due to the chronic political disunity in which Germany was left by the events and policies (or lack of policy) of the later Middle Ages. England and Sweden became Protestant countries; Spain, France and Italy remained Catholic ones; Hungary, at first protestantized, was won back completely to Catholicism in the counter-Reformation; Germany alone, with her mass of petty sovereignties and her all-but non-existent central authority, had to fall back on the solution of permanent religious partition and the principle of *cuius regio eius religio* which, of course, did not bring religious toleration within the separate principalities with it. An historian of Germany (Kurt Reinhardt)[1] who is also a good Catholic, has recently asserted that the fatal consequences of Luther's movement was the division of the German Nation into antagonistic camps—intellectual, social and political. This is hardly fair, because Germany was already divided before Luther laid his reforming hands on her. The link of a common confession and a single religious head had not sufficed to hold Germany together during the Middle Ages—indeed that same religious head had from time to time actively assisted in her disintegration. While Luther's creation of the Protestant alternative can hardly be said to have brought anything but further disunity to Germany in the political sphere, it is the pot calling the kettle black for him to be accused of *creating* this disunity. Furthermore, Germany achieved political unification in the nineteenth century while remaining part Protestant and part Catholic, and admitting the existence of other sects and religions as well. It is true that Bismarck, who did not 'want to go to Canossa', always treated religious matters with kid gloves on after his experience in the *Kulturkampf*, but by that time they were at least capable of being dealt with that way. In the days of Luther and right up to the Treaty of Westphalia, it was a free-for-all with bare fists.

The Reformation was for Germans a profound religious experience, even though many of its immediate

[1] In *Germany: 2000 Years* (Bruce, Milwaukee, 1950).

consequences there were of a secular nature. It did not give them unity or create a German nation comparable to the other 'New Monarchies', but, as has been seen, it brought Germany back into the main stream of European and world history.

CHAPTER VI

GERMANY AND THE RENAISSANCE

THE tide of the Renaissance did not cross the Alps until late in the fifteenth century, whereas that century as a whole, the *quattrocento*, is the great period of the Renaissance in Italy, where many of its manifestations were already evident in the fourteenth, in the work of Petrarch and his contemporaries.

The force of the Renaissance burst upon Germany not only late but slowly. Already by the middle of the fifteenth century Gutenberg was printing books with movable type (his Bible, printed by this means, was published about 1452), but the greatest writers of the German and northern Renaissance such as Erasmus and Reuchlin, and its greatest artists, such as Dürer and Holbein, flourished at the turn of the fifteenth into the sixteenth century. As an educational movement the German Renaissance had its roots in the foundation of the first universities on German and imperial soil in the second half of the fourteenth century (Prague in 1348 was the first, followed by Vienna in 1365 and Heidelberg in 1386). The Emperor Charles IV, the founder of Prague University, has been called 'the father of German humanism'. Further universities continued to be founded, and to contribute to the revival of classical learning, all through the fifteenth century, while the secular courts of Württemberg, Saxony, Brandenburg and the Palatinate, the ecclesiastical states such as Mainz under Archbishop Albrecht, as well as the more important south German cities such as Augsburg and Nürnberg were also centres of humanistic culture. Yet early in the sixteenth century humanism as a force was to be split and dissipated by the Reformation, which it aided mightily at first but from which it afterwards tended to recoil. Erasmus (who died in 1536) never went over to the Reformed religion, though he approved of many of Luther's earlier actions. The new universities of the sixteenth century were founded as either Catholic universities (such as Dillingen in 1519, Würzburg in 1582 and Graz in 1580) or as Protestant universities (such as Marburg in 1527, Jena in 1558 and Giessen in 1607—the year before the Protestant League). It was to be a long time before any one university was able to contain alongside each other both a Catholic and a Protestant theological faculty, but, nevertheless, in the fifteenth and sixteenth centuries the older universities such as Heidelberg, Erfurt and Basel modernized and humanized their medieval scholastic curricula, and this movement spread down to the schools as well. In particular, historical studies flourished in the fifteenth century as never before. It was the century that created the Barbarossa myth (originally associated not with Frederick I but with Frederick II) and added 'of the German Nation' to the title of the Holy Roman Emperor. The persistent antiquarianism of the Emperor Maximilian I, 'the last of the Knights', was a byword, and the remarkable set of bronze statues which he commissioned and which survive to this day in the Hofkirche in Innsbruck bear mute and impressive testimony to this craze. There, surrounding the kneeling figure of the Emperor himself, are King Arthur, Theodoric the Ostrogoth and twenty-six other figures, all in the costume or armour of the high Middle Ages, armed *cap-à-pie*, brandishing or leaning on their swords. The amount of historical research, or imagination, that went into the planning as well as the execution of this group, must have been very considerable. The equally famous stone statues in the cathedral at Naumburg, belonging to the thirteenth century, are portrait-statues of contemporaries, but this is a gallery of ancestors as Maximilian and his artists imagined and idealized them—in a way in which the Middle Ages could not have done.

More and more in German humanistic writings, even before the full impact of the Renaissance had been felt north of the Alps, did the terms *Germany* and *German* and *the German nation* appear, with at first a nationalistic undertone that had become an overtone well before the death of Maximilian in 1519. The phrase 'of the German nation' thus came readily to the pen of Martin Luther when he wrote his famous *Appeal* in 1521, in the way it could not have done to a controversialist of the early fifteenth century, or if he had used it, he would have been thinking of 'nation' in a much more limited sense, such as that of the 'nations' among the students in the late medieval universities. To the extent that Luther's Reformation was a German national revolt against the domination of a foreign Pope in Italy, it used verbal and emotional weapons sharpened at the courts of the fifteenth-century emperors, culminating in the remarkable galaxy of scholars, painters and poets which surrounded Maximilian. From the *Gravamina of the German Nation* (an early complaint against papal exactions) of 1456, through *The German Theology* of 1497 (which Luther re-edited in 1516) to the *Appeal to the Christian Nobility of the German Nation* of 1521, the *German Mass* of 1525 and the complete German version of the Bible published in 1534, the thread of national pride and feeling (mixed as it is with religious misgivings and experience) is a strong and broadening one. It is inconceivable that the Lutheran Reformation in Germany could have taken the form or acquired the momentum that it did but for its debt to, and its borrowing from, German humanism and the German Renaissance, which preceded it but which had not yet spent their force when Luther nailed up his *Ninety-Five Theses*.

It is perhaps symptomatic of this grand alliance of the Renaissance and the Reformation in Germany (although they were to fall apart before the end) that Hans Sachs, the quintessence of the bourgeois folk-poets known as the Meistersingers (successors to the courtly *Minnesänger* early in the fifteenth century), who applied guild rules to versification, should have promptly gone over to the Reformed faith and have called Martin Luther 'the nightingale of Wittenberg' as early as 1523. This was even more significant (for the Meistersingers sprang from the common people and not from either the cloister or the university) than the sympathy expressed for Luther's ideas by such typical Renaissance scholars as Erasmus, Ulrich von Hutton and Reuchlin.

CHAPTER VII

GERMANY AND THE *AUFKLÄRUNG*

THE fact that historians generally refer to the Age of Enlightenment of the seventeenth and the eighteenth century by its German name, the *Aufklärung*, whereas the *Renaissance* is usually given its French title, indicates in itself that the Germans and Germany must have participated more prominently in the former movement. Indeed, except in the earlier (seventeenth century) stages, they played a leading part in it, whereas their role in the Renaissance, which came at the end of a period of anarchy and political disunion in Germany, was never more than a minor one.

Indeed, but for the ravages of the Thirty Years War, Germany would probably have played as conspicuous a part in the seventeenth-century beginnings of the *Aufklärung* as did France. The limelight of European civilization was 'hogged' by the court of Louis XIV in the great palace he built for himself at Versailles until the beginning of the eighteenth century, when the sun of the *roi soleil* was beginning to set. Louis, and his armies, also had seen to it that rivals to Versailles did not have much chance of developing too soon on German soil. In 1689, for instance, advancing across the Rhine, and devastating the Palatinate as he went, he burnt the city of Heidelberg, capital of the Elector Palatine, and demolished its great castle and palace by charges of gunpowder placed inside its buildings. Before Versailles was built this had been the most magnificent palace north of the Alps. Its ruins are still impressive.

The period of art and architecture and of culture known as Baroque bridges the gap between the classical revival of the Renaissance and the new classical revival of the *Aufklärung*. Baroque was the product of the impact of humanism and Renaissance ideas upon late medieval Gothic, and represents a compromise between the high Middle Ages and the high Renaissance. It is associated in its rise with the Roman Catholic revival or restoration —called by Protestants the 'counter-Reformation'—and it flourished more in southern (Italy and Spain) than in northern Europe, its first great achievement being the ornamentation of St. Peter's at Rome. Nevertheless, many examples of Baroque appeared in Germany, particularly in Catholic Austria, but also in such states as Bavaria, Saxony and the Palatinate. A modified or 'northern' Baroque also developed in Prussia, particularly in and around the new capital of Berlin—as in the Old Museum, the Opera House and the Schloss. Baroque architecture, on the other hand, never flourished to any extent in France, and the palace-builders of Versailles were not influenced by it. They took their inspiration directly from Renaissance classicism, although France had remained a Catholic country.

The 'High Baroque' period was approximately from A.D. 1675 to 1725, and late Baroque was modified and adapted into the more fancy 'Rococo' (used at Sans Souci in Potsdam by Frederick the Great), which overlapped the new classical revival of the period of the enlightened despots, and the 'palladian' style in architecture so beloved by Thomas Jefferson. The Royal Palace at Schönbrunn in Vienna gives many evidences of this overlapping of styles, plus new and exotic influences, such as that of

Chinoiserie (or mock-oriental) to which Maria Theresa was susceptible.

Though Baroque architecture was 'received' in some parts of Europe, and rejected in others—in the east particularly, where Protestantism and its offshoot Puritanism had gained the firmest hold—the Baroque fashion of the periwig and the hoop-skirt dominated courts and courtiers everywhere, although the austere Frederick William I of Prussia banned it for his army and introduced a Chinese-type pigtail, or *Zopf*, instead. The *Zopf*, at first looked upon as barbaric, was more hygenic and easier to dress, and by about the middle of the eighteenth century had driven out the periwig altogether. Nevertheless, *Zopftstil* remained a term of reproach or denigration up to the Revolution, just as *Biedermeier* was to become after 1815.

The seventeenth-century precursors of the literary and philosophical enlightenment in Germany were those who preached a new rationalism. Thus Leibnitz (who died in 1714), one of whose greatest achievements was the founding of the Prussian Academy of Science in 1700 in Berlin, has been described as a 'typical Baroque philosopher', but his influence on the eighteenth-century *Aufklärung* was great. So indeed was that of Pufendorf (who had died in 1694). Both of these men sketched a blue-print of behaviour for the 'enlightened despot' whose duty it was to bring happiness to his people, and both preached an optimistic view of history and of the universe that had been missing from the ideas of most Reformation and counter-Reformation thinkers. While not in any sense anti-religious, as were many of the eighteenth-century French and German *philosophes*, Leibnitz and Pufendorf had a secular and rational approach even to religious problems. A more 'popular' type of philosopher, Christian Wolff (he died in 1754), who has been described as the real 'father of the *Aufklärung*', pushed their rational approach even farther, and with his contemporary Thomasius, 'the apostle of Common Sense'—who insisted on lecturing in the German language in the Latin-dominated German universities of his day—performed a similar function to that of homespun philosophers such as Benjamin Franklin and Thomas Paine in the Anglo-American culture sphere. Wolff, expelled from the University of Halle by the philistine Frederick William I, was brought back in triumph to be its head by Frederick the Great after his accession. Halle was already the centre of the German educational *Aufklärung*, and freedom of teaching had been proclaimed there as early as 1711.

The full impact of the Enlightenment did not hit Germany until such unenlightened rulers as Frederick William I and the Emperor Charles VI had disappeared from the scene (both of them died in the year 1740) to be succeeded by those typical 'enlightened despots' Frederick the Great and Maria Theresa. These rulers, by giving their patronage to the new trend, allowed Germany to match France and Switzerland and Britain (where 'enlightenment' had been growing in strength ever since the 'Glorious Revolution' of 1688) in her worship of the 'religion' of reason. These new rulers corresponded with Voltaire and the French encyclopaedists, read Locke and Montesquieu and lent inspiration to a new generation of writers and philosophers, who had they but known it, were in their turn to question the very basis of enlightened despotism and throw another ideological bridge across to a new age of revolutionary upheaval and romantic revival. Such men were Lessing (1729–81), Kant (1724–1804) and Herder (1744–1803), all of them children of the *Aufklärung*, and among its most finished and influential exponents. These men, and especially Lessing and Kant, brought Germany for the first time since the days of Luther (with the exception of that versatile genius Leibnitz) to the centre of the western world's intellectual stage. Before his death Emmanuel Kant, the sage of Königsberg, was a world figure more highly respected than 'Old Fritz' himself had ever been, and Lessing was to lend inspiration both to the classical and to the romantic revivals of German literature. Lessing, in his *Minna von Barnhelm* (1763) produced the first modern German comedy with a contemporary theme, and in *Nathan the Wise* (1779) a plea for religious and racial toleration of the most comprehensive sort, providing a refutation of the ideas of Hitler (who banned the play after he came to power) nearly 150 years before *Mein Kampf* was written. Lessing's plays and some of his other writings can still be read with pleasure, and have had a wide appeal ever since they were published. His predecessor Gottsched (1700–76), so long the literary arbiter of Germany, is now almost unread and is virtually unreadable. The gospel of enlightenment which Lessing preached in his works, and particularly in his last great essay *The Education of the Human Race* (1780), was a rounded philosophy that struck out in many directions. It had stimulated the young poets of the *Storm and Stress* (an incandescent outburst of literary activity of a new type, highly emotional yet not 'romantic') in the 1770's, and influenced Schiller's seminal work on *The Stage as Moral Instruction* (1784) and his plays—the first of which, *The Robbers* (1777), had been written during Lessing's lifetime and first played in the year of his death in 1781—as much as did the ideas of Emmanuel Kant. Goethe, too, acknowledged the extent of Lessing's influence upon him.

Herder, with his interest in the popular literature and songs of Germany's past, while he owed much to the re-discovery of the works of the *Minnesänger*, and the *Niebelungenlied*, by earlier eighteenth-century German scholars—was the inventor of the concept of *Volksgeist*, which played so big a part in the development of both the 'romantic' and the 'historical' schools in nineteenth-century Germany, and incidentally of German national feeling even in its extreme forms. Unlike Lessing, Herder was made a cult of by the National-Socialists, who over-used and misused the word *Volk* to which he had given its first significance in connection with the German national heritage. His influence on the romantic revival was great.

The great literary and intellectual efflorescence of the German mind which lasted from the beginning of the *Sturm und Drang* in 1770 to the death of Goethe in 1832 produced many remarkable works from a number of many-sided men. It repudiated much of the coldness and formalism of the *Aufklärung*, but it could not have occurred without the *Aufklärung* coming first, just as in politics and government the age of the enlightened despots had to precede the outbreak of the French Revolution. The men of the *Aufklärung* and the Storm and Stress, and the early romantic school in Germany, in their writings up to the end of the eighteenth century were, unlike their French contemporaries, singularly uninterested in practical politics and in the re-founding of the state on a more popular basis, for their sphere of activity was the *Kleinstaat*. Goethe in Weimar, Schiller in Württemberg (and finally Weimar also), lived under the patronage of benevolent despots. They wanted neither to *écraser l'infâme* like Voltaire, nor to break men's political chains (which they hardly felt) or the social caste system into which they had been born (they both let themselves be en-nobled), as Rousseau had advocated. The political complacency of the leaders of German thought and creative writing during the second half of the eighteenth century helps to explain the coolness with which the French and American Revolutions were received by them after the first raptures. These men were applying their great talents to other things. Nobody could accuse Lessing and Goethe and Schiller and Kant and Beethoven of not believing in the liberation of the human spirit, and, indeed, those of them who survived into the years of the Napoleonic tyranny over Europe protested vehemently against it, but they did not instinctively think or act along political lines. Intelligent foreign observers like Mirabeau, Madame de Stael and James Boswell realized this defect in the German literary and intellectual giants of their age—who were blissfully unaware of it. They themselves did not reckon the cost of leaving it to lesser men with cruder ideas and methods to lead Germany and the German spirit out of the ivory tower. The cost included the humiliations of Jena and Austerlitz and Tilsit, the frustrations of 1848, the 'blood and iron' of Bismarck, and the national catastrophes of 1918 and 1945. The political influence of Lessing and Kant, and of Goethe and Schiller was remarkably slight when compared with their literary fame. This was, of course, a reflection of the condition of the country in which they were born. The political challenge to 'men of light and leading' such as existed in Paris and London, in Boston and Philadelphia around the 1770's and 1780's, did not present itself in Vienna and Berlin, in Frankfurt and Dresden, or even in Stuttgart and Weimar.

CHAPTER VIII

GERMANY AND THE FRENCH REVOLUTION

THE political fragmentation of eighteenth-century Germany, and the lack of political interests and ideals in her intellectual leaders, resulted in her reaction to the outbreak of the French Revolution being a very confused one indeed. She was not ready for the news that came from Paris, and each new turn that the Revolution took in France added to the confusion in the Rhineland and beyond.

For an Assembly of Estates to insist upon its right to be revived and consulted and to state its grievances in the name of the people it represented was nothing novel for Germany. The Estates of Württemberg had recently vindicated its ancient rights and had succeeded in tempering the despotism of the formidable Elector, Duke Karl Eugen. Reforms of the sort that the *Cahiers* had demanded in France had long since been introduced in a number of German states, while the young Duke of Weimar had called in the even younger Goethe (who had a dilettante interest in politics but no interest whatsoever in representative government) in 1775 to help him to rule his diminutive state as so benevolent a despotism that the twin tidal waves of the Revolution and Napoleon were to fail to shake his rule or arouse his dutiful subjects. The 'Poo-Bah' Goethe, chief minister, minister of finance, president of the chamber, privy councillor, director of the Residence theatre, arbiter of fashion and of taste and presiding genius over a sort of latter-day Court of Love, rode out the Revolution and the era of Napoleon at Weimar with effortless complacency. 'How much is this the greatest event in the history of the world' he exclaimed on hearing the news of the French victory at Valmy, but he is not known to have followed up that remark by any other action or reaction. In 1808 he remarked of Napoleon 'that man is too much for us', implying that the Germans and Germany had best lie low under the tyrant's heel. He took, one is not surprised to learn, no part in the Liberation movement, though he applauded it discreetly from afar as soon as it had Napoleon on the run out of Germany. If the leading literary and intellectual figure of the day behaved like this, why should lesser men react to the French Revolution with more spirit? Most of them did not. Schiller, dying in 1805, escaped having to define his attitude towards the Liberation. (He had spent his last years studying the history of the Thirty Years War and giving it imperishable dramatic form.) Fichte, who played such a big part in stimulating the spirit of the Liberation, was one of the few German intellectuals who had welcomed the French Revolution and who had continued to regard its progress with any enthusiasm. Most of them had been frightened off by the execution of King Louis XVI, by the Terror, or by Edmund Burke. Görres, a Rhinelander who had welcomed occupation and annexation by France (as did many of his fellow Rhinelanders, notably the 'separatist' Georg Forster of Mainz), changed his mind, too, under the pressure of the Bonapartist dictatorship, and ended up as a German patriot of an extreme type. Thus, those Germans who welcomed the Revolution, and who were not scared into opposition by its early excesses, were later to be driven into opposition to what Napoleon turned it into, and to recognize the implications of the Napoleonic menace to the integrity and future of their country. Few of them, on the other hand, realized what contributions Napoleon was unwittingly making[1] to the solution of the German problem; nor that he was turning this German problem into a European problem. Indeed, hardly any of them realized that a 'German problem' as such existed at all. There were, of course, in their eyes, Prussian problems and Austrian problems, Saxon problems and Bavarian problems, and so on. Karl August and Goethe had their problems in Weimar, beyond the narrow confines of which they did not look more often than they were forced to do. Join the Confederation of the Rhine? Furnish conscripts for the *Grande Armée*? Pay tribute that would end up as gilt on the dome of the Invalides? Why, yes! Anything for peace and quiet! Then one could return to the current dramatic production and the current court flirtation, issue a new decree, plan a new water-garden, do a dissection, make an astronomical observation, write a few more lines of *Faust* and go to bed (preferably not alone) happy and contented.

It is, nevertheless, possible to judge Goethe too harshly. His closest attention to political affairs was concentrated into the ten years following his call to Weimar in 1774, and he had 'relapsed into literature' as his main concern before the French Revolution broke out. In his indifference to the German national feeling he was simply not in advance of his age, an age in which 'the Nationalists were voices crying in the wilderness, Particularism was the instincts of the masses, Cosmopolitanism the creed of the élite' (G. P. Gooch). While Nicolai was calling a German

[1] See pp. 112–14.

nation 'a political monstrosity', Schiller was writing as 'a citizen of the world who serves no prince' and Lessing was repudiating the significance of national boundaries in politics, it would have demanded superhuman powers such as even Goethe did not possess to espouse nineteenth-century ideas in the eighteenth century, a century in which, like the seventeenth, 'Germany suffered from an almost complete dearth of political thought and public opinion' (R. Pascal). The impact of Rousseau's writings upon Germany, though enormous, was more an emotional than a political one, and was greater upon the romantic school which flourished only after the French Revolution had broken out, than upon the *Sturm und Drang* and the later writer of the *Aufklärung*. The German *Aufklärung* did not question the principles of enlightened despotism, though (like Lessing) some of its members questioned whether some of the German states (such as the Prussia of Frederick the Great) were as enlightened as they professed to be.

While there is general agreement that the Germany of 1789, particularist and unpolitical as it was so overwhelmingly, was totally unprepared for such a world-shaking event as the French Revolution, historians and publicists continue to differ widely regarding the extent of the influence of the French Revolution upon Germany, and the rapidity with which this influence was felt. Haller, taking an extreme point of view, denies that 1789 opened any new epoch for Germany and thinks that two whole generations elapsed before any open imitation of the French example was seen in action on German soil. He stresses the importance of the *rapprochement* that was caused between Austria and Prussia (at loggerheads since 1740) by the situation in France (Austria's ally since 1756 up to the eclipse of the political and social system of Louis XVI and Marie Antoinette), an alliance that was to persist throughout the régime of Metternich, with Prussia as the junior partner right up to the end of the reign of Frederick William IV. Gooch, on the other hand, lays great stress on the destruction of the age-old political framework of Germany as a result of the impact of the French Revolution and of Napoleon between the years 1792 and 1806 and on the renaissance of Prussian power after 1806 as an equally direct consequence of these forces. These two consequences were to be dominating factors in the history of Germany throughout the nineteenth century, from which Prussia emerged as a major force in Europe and a united Germany as a great power in the world. If the French Revolution had not broken out when it did or taken the course that it did, modern Germany would not have taken the shape it assumed, even if it would have taken definite shape at all.

The historians may continue to argue about 'speed and extent', but it is more than clear that the men of the Liberation—Fichte, Stein, Hardenberg, Scharnhort, Arndt, Jahn, Görres and others—were pursued and enflamed by the whips and scorpions that the French Revolution unleashed. Germany and the Germans had their noses rubbed into the stern realities of the modern world during those two decades after 1789 as never before. Georg Forster of Mainz expressed the wish that Germany could warm herself at the flames of the French Revolution without being burnt. This wish (despite the assumption of G. P. Gooch to the contrary) can hardly be said to have been fulfilled.

CHAPTER IX

GERMANY AND THE EXPANSION OF EUROPE

THE Germans, who were the most active and successful as colonizers of all the peoples of Europe in the Middle Ages, were sadly left behind in the new outburst of colonial expansion which occurred at the beginning of modern times. The chronic state of disunity into which Germany fell after the middle of the thirteenth century not only accounted for the fading away of her eastward expansion into the Baltic lands, and her failure to stem the advance of the Ottoman Turks into the Danube valley, in the fifteenth century, but it meant that the German states and cities were in no way able to emulate Portugal, Spain, England, France and the United Netherlands in the sixteenth and seventeenth centuries in opening up a new world overseas. It is true that German scholars and navigators participated as individuals in the work of the era of discovery, and German geographers and map-makers were particularly active in sifting and making use of the new knowledge of the world that the voyagers brought back. But no German state or court (although the Emperor Charles V, in his other capacity as King of Spain, was acquiring a great Empire across the Atlantic and even the Pacific) sent out or subsidized expeditions aiming to establish colonies overseas.

Until late in the seventeenth century emigration overseas on the part of Germans was negligible, and when refugees from the devastated Palatinate and elsewhere in western Germany did begin to reach North America, they went to the British mainland colonies (notably Pennsylvania) and not to any area over which a German state or ruler could continue to exercise sovereignty. As Germans, therefore, they were lost. They clung to their German speech and ways for a long time—Benjamin Franklin in the middle of the eighteenth century found it profitable to publish a newspaper for them in the German language—but they became British subjects and (after 1776) American citizens, and very few of them ever returned to the lands of their birth. The same process of alienation occurred in the cases of the relatively few Germans who emigrated up to the end of the eighteenth century to other parts of the world.

When a new German national feeling had been aroused by the events of the era of Liberation, coming, as it did, hot on the heels of the American and French Revolutions, this failure to establish colonies abroad, this loss of man-power to regions overseas, controlled by non-German states, began to arouse in many Germans a feeling of frustration and helplessness. The rich plums among overseas possessions were all being plucked by others. Little Holland had acquired a great Empire in the Far East; France, after losing her foothold in North America and India in the eighteenth century, turned to North and Central Africa and to farther Asia in the nineteenth and established a second colonial empire there; Britain, despite the break-away of the United States of America went on to acquire a new Empire in Africa and Asia to add to the very considerable territories she had retained of her first Empire; even Russia, though her sphere of expansion was not technically 'overseas' (apart from a few bases on the Pacific coast of North America), began to open up and exploit a vast new 'colonial' region in Siberia from the seventeenth century onwards; only Spain and Portugal relapsed into insignificance as colonial powers, and even these two countries, in the wreckage of their once great empires, retained more overseas territory than any German state had ever possessed—for not one of them possessed any at all. Only Italy, that other 'geographical expression', was comparable to Germany in her chronic state of non-participation in these new colonial endeavours. Both countries had to wait until their political unification had been achieved in the 1860's before they could think at all integrally or effectively of colonial expansion, and by that time only the 'leavings' of the other powers were available—territories so unattractive, so remote or so insignificant that it had not seemed profitable for anyone else to occupy or lay claim to them.

German states and rulers had, before Bismarck's unification, toyed from time to time with the idea of acquiring colonies—Prussia was the most active in this connection—but nothing had come of it. The Great Elector's African plans proved very costly and their results were only transitory. Frederick the Great had concluded a treaty with the newly independent United States, and had exchanged ambassadors with the Continental Congress, but he does not seem to have considered attempting to secure a colony for Prussia in the Americas. When, as late as 1843, a sadly harassed Mexico offered its province of Upper California (already menaced by independent-minded immigrants from the United States and Europe) to the government of Prussia for the bargain price of six million dollars—mindful no doubt that France had sold Louisiana in 1803 for fifteen million dollars, but that she, Mexico, had lost Texas in

1835 without any compensation at all—the Prussian Foreign Ministry advised a timid king against snapping up the bargain, for its acceptance might have led to a breach of good relations with the United States, a country which only twenty years before had made its position towards any such transaction crystal-clear by the enunciation of the Monroe Doctrine. No other German state ever had an opportunity to secure an American colony at a bargain or any other price. When a Habsburg Archduke went out to Mexico to try to make himself its emperor in the sixties, it was not under the flag of his brother the Austrian Emperor that he embarked upon his ill-starred adventure, but under the wing of the much more tattered eagle of the *parvenu* French Emperor Napoleon III.

Even after the unification of 1871, Bismarck (who was not by inclination a colonialist and considered it his main task to consolidate Germany's hard-won position in Europe rather than to embark upon risky adventures overseas) resisted the growing demand that Imperial Germany should safeguard and extend her trading interests abroad by acquiring colonies until 1884, when he made South-West Africa a German protectorate, and annexed Togoland and the Cameroons in Central Africa. This proved to be the beginning of a slippery slope down which Bismarck and his successors progressed until they had acquired territories in East Africa, New Guinea and the South Seas (the Marshall Islands) in 1885; further Pacific Island—by purchase from Spain, who had just lost the Philippines to the United States—in 1899 (the Carolines, the Mariannas and Palau) and—by establishing a protectorate over the greater part of Samoa—in 1900. A foothold on the mainland of China was secured in 1898 by Germany taking over Kiachow as a treaty port, to which Tsingtau was added, after the Boxer Riots, in 1900.

Germany, in some fifteen years, had secured overseas possessions or protectorates covering over a million square miles in extent and containing a population of some twelve million souls, but these were mainly backward territories, 'ripe for development' only if vast sums of money could be sunk into them. Few, if any, of them were suitable for settlement by Germans from the Fatherland, and only attracted a handful of officials, soldiers and traders. Even by the year 1914 the German overseas Empire was far short of being a paying proposition, comparable to the Empires of Britain, France and the Netherlands or even of that other late-comer on the colonial scene, Belgium, whose king (Leopold II) had picked up in the Congo a vast and rich territory, which, by the turn of the century, he and his associates (it had not yet been taken over by the Belgian state) were exploiting with great efficiency and ruthlessness and to their very considerable profit.

As Bismarck had feared, Germany's new colonial policy soon caused friction between her and the other powers whose spheres of 'influence' and of 'legitimate aspiration' tended to overlap those in which she was now operating, and when her colonialists and militarists succeeded in persuading the government in Berlin to build a large and powerful fleet after 1898 to help protect and (if possible) extend Germany's overseas interests, an intense rivalry quickly grew up between the German and the British Empires and the good relations which Bismarck had so skilfully maintained were shattered. Britain was soon to be driven into the arms of her old rivals and former enemies France and Russia (in the dual and triple *ententes* of 1904 and 1907) largely through her resentment of Germany's colonial and naval ambitions, and an atmosphere of mutual suspicion was built up which contributed a great deal towards causing the international catastrophe of 1914.

Nobody can blame Imperial Germany (the international situation having been what it was at the end of the nineteenth century) for deciding that she needed a powerful navy, although her refusal to consider seriously the possibility of an understanding with Britain, and her extremely unco-operative attitude towards the peace movement associated with the Hague Conferences can be criticized more easily. But it was her dog-in-the-manger attitude of interfering in the affairs and spheres of influence of the other powers without prospect of any real advantage to herself which was the worst feature of her foreign policy under William II and which eventually lost her the friendship and confidence of all the other powers that mattered. Unable effectively to interfere on behalf of the Boers against Britain, William nevertheless sent his notorious letter of encouragement to President Kruger, and then several years later boasted (in the *Daily Telegraph* interview of 1908) that he had also advised the British on how best to win the war in South Africa! Chagrined at France's assumption of a protectorate over Morocco (to which Britain had agreed in return for a free hand in Egypt), William, posing as the friend and protector of Moslems everywhere, intervened there on three separate occasions—by a speech in Tangiers in 1903, by an appeal to the Hague Court in 1908 and by a gunboat (the *Panther*) in 1911—on each occasion risking the outbreak of international war without obtaining any substantial advantage and only minor 'compensations'. The Berlin-Bagdad-Basra railway agreement with Turkey of 1902 was likewise a gesture of defiance which Germany was not really in a position to back up, and which did more than anything else to draw Britain and Russia, those traditional rivals in the Middle East, together in the agreement of 1907, which defined their spheres of influence there and left nothing over for Germany. The same thing was happening elsewhere (in the Balkans for instance), and everywhere Germany appeared as the disturber of the peace, prepared to go to the most reckless lengths for very small gains in prestige or territory—such as the additional slice of the Cameroons she obtained as a sop in the settlement of the Algeciras crisis of 1911. This was her last colonial acquisition before she was to lose all her colonies and the capital she had sunk into them at the treaty of Versailles after her defeat in 1918.

Her colonies had never been a source of profit to her and had infinitely complicated her international position, but long before 1914 their retention and exploitation had become to Germany a vital matter of national prestige out of all relation to their true worth and potentialities. After losing their colonies the Germans felt almost as badly about those tracts of uninhabited Kalahari desert in South-West Africa, and those strings of barren Pacific atolls as she did about Alsace-Lorraine, Eupen, Malmedy, Upper Silesia and the Polish corridor. When Adolf Hitler came to power in 1933 he put the recovery of Germany's lost colonies to the forefront of his propaganda and his promises, although he was later to express willingness to call the whole campaign off in exchange for a free hand in central and eastern Europe!

Germany has emerged from the Second World War, as she did from the First, without a square mile of overseas territory. It remains to be seen whether she will be able to steel herself to face with equanimity remaining permanently in this position—a position which scarcely bothered any German before 1871, but which Germans came, after 1918 (although their first colony had then been acquired as recently as thirty-three years before), to regard as the quintessence of national humiliation.

CHAPTER X

GERMAN EMIGRATION: EUROPEAN AND OVERSEAS

SINCE the days of their immigration into the land which became Germany, the Germanic peoples, who had participated in the *Völkerwanderung* and had at last settled down in the valleys of the Rhine, the Weser, the Elbe, the Main and the upper Danube, have expanded beyond the confines of this area on four separate occasions.

First of all they went as warriors and settlers (rather on the model of the Roman 'colonists') into the series of Marks or new frontier provinces beyond the Elbe and on the middle Danube. This expansion resulted in the greatest permanent extension of Germany's political boundaries, for it advanced them eastwards to and beyond the Oder and into the middle Danube and gave them bastions from which they could hold in check non-Germanic peoples, such as the Magyars, who were now pressing in from the east.

The second great wave of German expansion, about which a good deal has already been said, was less permanent in its results. In the twelfth, thirteenth and fourteenth centuries it advanced the German 'frontier of settlement' north-eastwards up the southern shores of the Baltic as far as Esthonia under the powerful military protection of the Teutonic Knights and the Knights of the Sword and under the economic wing of the Hanseatic League. But, of this area (beyond the Oder river), only

East Prussia was thoroughly Germanized and even that province was not comprehended within the Holy Roman Empire, and, when the Slavonic peoples counter-attacked in the fifteenth century, Esthonia, Latvia and Lithuania were lost and the powerful new Slavonic state of Poland came to dominate the valley of the Vistula river. The German settlers did not all withdraw from the Baltic provinces when the power of the Teutonic Knights and of the Hanse collapsed there, but they became the subjects of Slavonic princes. These 'Baltic' Germans (concentrated mainly but not exclusively in the towns of the area) became the first 'splinters' (as Hitler was to call them) of German culture, the first 'islands' of German speech (*Sprachinseln*) to be split off politically from the great body of Germany. Comparable islands of German settlement and speech farther south in Bohemia and Hungary, which also date from the later Middle Ages, are different from the Baltic 'splinters' in that the German settlers there alienated themselves from Germany politically from the beginning and deliberately accepted the sovereignty over them of non-German rulers in return for land and the promises of prosperity. This was notably the case in Transylvania, whence the 'Siebenburgen' Germans transplanted German civilization most comprehensively, but where they were as completely cut off from any political connection with Germany as the 'Pennsylvania Germans' who went to America in the eighteenth century were to be.

The third great wave of German emigration began indeed with this settlement in the British North American colonies in the late seventeenth and the eighteenth centuries, after several centuries during which the population of Germany had not been expanding rapidly enough to make the urge to emigrate very strong, and during which the two great demographic catastrophes of the Black Death and the Thirty Years War had occurred. During these centuries Germans did, of course, leave their native land, but only as individuals and families and small groups. There was nothing approaching a mass emigration. Indeed, Germany was, on the other hand, receiving immigrants from other countries, the most famous group of these being the Huguenots who came from France into a number of German Protestant states, and into Brandenburg-Prussia in particular, after the revocation of the Edict of Nantes.

The third wave, which began to gather only towards the end of the seventeenth century, was to be the most spectacular of all, for after sinking to small proportions during the Revolutionary and Napoleonic Wars, it rose to a high crest in the middle years of the nineteenth century (especially in the years immediately succeeding the revolutions of 1848) and remained considerable right up to the war of 1914. It was this emigration which took over six millions of Germans to new homes overseas between Louis XIV's devastation of the Palatinate in 1689—which helped to start the movement—and the German invasion of Belgium in 1914—which may be said to have marked its end. This was a larger number of people than the whole population of Germany in the early Middle Ages, and almost as many as had survived in that country after the Black Death. It was more, too, than the entire population of Prussia at the death of Frederick the Great. If every subject of Frederick had emigrated in the one year 1786 the effect upon the history of Germany, of America and of the world would of course have been different than of the same number of Germans leaving over a period of two and a half centuries at an average yearly rate of some 25,000—though in the year 1854 alone it was in fact nearly a quarter of a million and in 1884 just over that figure—but the total is nevertheless a very remarkable one, and its size has been a major factor in the development of modern Germany—and of the United States, to which country a majority of the emigrants went. This 'great emigration', therefore, merits further careful analysis.

The fourth wave of German emigration has taken place in our own time and has been of a most singular nature. Perhaps it should rather be described as a series of wavelets, or more in the nature of the effect of a large stone dropped into a deep pool, sending a series of concentric ripples to lap and to overlap its shores, setting up a counter-movement inwards towards the centre of the pool once more when the displaced volume of water pressed back into it.

From being among the most highly esteemed people on this earth before 1914, welcome everywhere as settlers for their skill, their industrious habits, their culture and their high level of education and intelligence, the Germans suddenly found themselves, after 1918, far less welcome than before as overseas settlers. They had never migrated in any considerable numbers to Germany's own somewhat meagre and inhospitable colonies—which were now in any case lost—and in the great 'wide open spaces' of North and South America, of South Africa and of Australasia they were now classed as 'enemy aliens' or—hardly less acceptably—'ex-enemy aliens' and very noticeably cold-shouldered. This chilly atmosphere continued at any rate up to the improvement in Germany's international status and her re-acceptance as a member of the family of nations after the Locarno Treaties of 1925. Meanwhile, the 'National Origins' provisions of the United States immigration law of 1924 (replacing the temporary 'Quota' Restrictions of 1917) had all but closed the door of that country to natives of Germany, who now once again, with the Hohenzollern Empire in ruins and ever-mounting inflation replacing pre-war economic prosperity by post-war instability and unemployment, were anxious to emigrate in large numbers. They were restricted to 26,000 in any one year, and until 1930 many would-be emigrants to the United States either had to stay at home or were deflected to Brazil or Australia, where they were more welcome. After 1930 the world depression, which hit the United States almost as heavily as it did Germany, had the effect of making that country cease, for a few years, to be 'the land of opportunity' and the quota was not filled. Indeed more Germans were returning to Germany from America each year in the thirties than were emigrating. This had never happened before. To some of them, and particularly if they had retained their German citizenship, it was represented by National-Socialist party propagandists to be their patriotic duty to return to Germany and participate in the new national 'awakening', and in particular they were encouraged to send back their sons of military age to swell Germany's manpower. Some German-Americans paid heed to this siren-song, but the vast majority did not.

At the same time there began a new political emigration out of Germany, comparable to that which had followed the failure of the revolutions of 1848. The persecuted Jews and the displaced liberals among the German intelligentsia departed in their thousands every year after 1933 and many more would have left had they possessed the means to do so. The loss to Germany was at least as serious as to France when Louis XIV had driven out the Huguenots. Among the many distinguished

Germans who emigrated during these years were Albert Einstein, the world-renowned physicist, and Thomas Mann, perhaps Germany's most distinguished literary figure. When Hitler annexed Austria in 1938, the great medical psychologist Siegmund Freud fled to England. Nearly every university in the free world took German scholars-in-exile on to its staff, very often to its great advantage. Great institutions like the Library of Congress in Washington, D.C., and the Institute for Advanced Studies at Princeton, found many positions for them. In the war of 1939–45 these men and women thus lent their ability and learning to the cause, not of Germany, but of Germany's enemies. Driving them into exile had been perhaps the most stupid act of a régime which prided itself on its cunning and efficiency.

When the Second World War came, despite the attempts made to bring back Germans from abroad (a notorious agreement between Hitler and Mussolini in 1939 had provided for the repatriation of the South-Tyrolese Germans who had been transferred from Austria to Italy in 1919) and despite the annexation of Austria, Bohemia and Moravia and other territories which could be made to work for the greater glory of the Third Reich, Germany was faced with a very serious manpower shortage, much greater even than that which had existed for her (up to the last year at least) of the First World War. To meet this shortage, over ten million foreign civilians were ordered or persuaded to enter Germany's factories and till her fields, quite apart from the many thousands of prisoners of war who were made use of in the same way. This was a forced migration which did not outlast Germany's collapse in 1945, but it was another example of the complicated alternation of wave and counter-wave which has already been described. The experience of these foreign workers, many of them living virtually in a state of slavery, was to build up a feeling of resentment and bitterness against everything German in the countries surrounding Germany that surpassed even the hatreds engendered by the First World War—a war in which Holland, Denmark and Norway, at least, had not been overrun.

Then with the peace came a new influx—the Germans fleeing before the Soviet Armies out of the 'East-Land' that Germany had won and held after so many centuries of struggle, and those other 'Germans' who had lived peaceably in Bohemia and Moravia, in Hungary and Rumania and the Balkans for hundreds of years, but who were now, on account of the use Hitler had made of them, regarded as a dangerous 'fifth column' constituting a menace to the integrity of any non-German state in which they resided. Some of these German-speaking communities had been removed even during the war—such as the Volga Germans, taken into Russia by Catherine the Great (herself a German princess), who were removed neck and crop by Stalin to a remote part of Siberia—but many of the remaining ones were dispersed (particularly in the countries immediately bordering on Germany) when the war was over, and the 'splinter-Germans' poured back into Germany in their hundreds of thousands, as 'expellees' (*Flüchtlinge*). By 1950, the West German Republic, as has been already noted,[1] contained twelve million *Flüchtlinge* (including those who had fled from the east zones of Germany occupied and administered by the Russians and the Poles).

Emigration out of Germany, therefore, except in its very first phase, which did advance the frontier of

[1] See p. 86.

Germany to the east and the south-east to a significant extent, has not been a movement bringing any great advantage to Germany herself. It has sometimes relieved population pressure and economic misery, but it has not built up the power and prestige and enhanced the name of Germany in the way that emigration from such countries as England and Holland has done for them. On balance Germany has lost more than she has gained from emigration and not one of the 'new Germanies' that have been established on foreign soil—in Transylvania, on the Volga, in Rio Grande do Sul in Brazil, in Pennsylvania, in Texas, in Missouri, in Wisconsin and elsewhere—has ever retained or established a state of political or economic dependence upon Germany. It has been one of the great tragedies of Germany's history that, since the later Middle Ages, she has suffered an almost continuous drain of human capital and ability, without receiving any of the compensations that came to such countries as Portugal and Spain, Britain, France and Holland in varying degrees as a result of their participation in the Age of Discovery (fifteenth and sixteenth centuries), the Age of Colonization (seventeenth and eighteenth centuries) and the Age of the Great Migrations (nineteenth and twentieth centuries). Above all, she has contributed manpower and ability she could ill spare to the building up of powerful new nations overseas, like the United States of America, Brazil, Argentina, Canada and Australia—countries which nearly all fought against her in the two World Wars of the present century. Highly as they have respected and cherished their German cultural heritage (and in some cases even retained their German speech, or—as in Pennsylvania and Rio Grande do Sul—a diluted form of it) they have nowhere, except in a few individual and isolated cases, retained a political loyalty to Germany which has come near to challenging their loyalty to the new country of their adoption. In the First World War German-Americans (directed and encouraged by the powerful German-American National Alliance) did everything possible to support the neutrality policy of the United States—and to prevent her from giving aid to the Allied and Associated Powers against Germany—up to President Wilson's declaration of war in April 1917. After that the vast majority of German-Americans merged themselves with other Americans in the war effort. At the beginning of the Second World War, because most German-Americans were anti-Nazi (whereas in 1914 they had been pro-Hohenzollern), the movement among Americans of German descent to prevent aid for Britain or to lend encouragement to Germany was of negligible proportions, and even before Pearl Harbour it had virtually disappeared in the eclipse of the comic-opera 'American-German People's League' (the notorious *Bund*) of Fritz Kühn, which had only attracted the approbation of America's fascist fringe. In both World Wars the German Government and people were saddened and perplexed by the relatively unresponsive attitude of Germans and the descendants of Germans who had migrated overseas towards the German national cause. But these Germans had emigrated to escape land-hunger, to escape military conscription, to escape political repression and religious persecution, to escape financial inflation and unemployment in the land of their birth. In the lands of their adoption most of them *had* escaped most of these evils. Why then should they look back upon Germany with any feeling of political obligation or social nostalgia? They found plenty that they did not like in their new world, but they had left behind them in the old even more that they disliked. Not all of them became cabinet ministers like Carl Schurz or United States senators like Robert Wagner, Congressmen like Lorenz Brentano, movie magnates like Carl Laemmle, professors of culture-history at Harvard like Kuno Francke, famous political cartoonists like Thomas Nast, presidents of the American Medical Association like Abraham Jacobi, founders of great industrial concerns like Heinrich Steinweg (Steinway pianos) and J. A. Faber (Faber pencils), not to mention the brewers of such beers as 'Pabst' and 'Schlitz' and the 'Budweiser' of Anhäuser-Busch, whose names have become household words. Many of these German emigrants have remained 'obscure men' in the United States, in Canada, in Australia, in Brazil, in Chile and elsewhere, but most of them led fuller and less frustrated lives than if they had remained behind in the Germany of the nineteenth and twentieth centuries. Some German emigrants did indeed hail the founding of the Bismarck-Hohenzollern Empire as the dawn of a new era and decided to return, either to live there permanently or on first visits to Germany in twenty-five or more years. Very few of them liked what they found there. Frederick Hecker, the exiled leader of the Baden Republican Revolution of 1848–49, on landing at Baltimore after several months in unified Germany in 1873, told reporters that it was 'more autocratic than the old Roman imperium', and William Rapp said in Chicago in 1874 that the new Germany 'does not conform to our ideals'. If such men could barely tolerate what Bismarck had to offer, it is small wonder that they (or their sons and grandsons) were even less impressed by the garish Imperial Germany of Bülow and William II, by the down-at-heel Republican Germany of Ebert and Hindenburg and by the barbarous Third Reich of Adolf Hitler!

For a century and a half Germany has been exporting her finest citizens and potential citizens to countries overseas and in most cases losing them altogether as Germans. While men like Lieber and Schurz, Hecker and Brentano, Einstein and Thomas Mann departed for ever, Germany finally fell into the hands of creatures of the stamp of Rosenberg and Ley, Goering and Goebbels, Himmler and Ribbentrop, Hitler himself and the unspeakable Streicher!

Germany today is overpopulated in the west and underpopulated in the east. This, if and when reunion is achieved, may allow her to strike a balance in the distribution of her population without recourse to large-scale emigration. But in any case she can never recover what she has lost already by emigration—voluntary or enforced—to countries better able to take care of her citizens than she was herself.

CHAPTER XI

CONCLUSION: GERMANY'S PLACE IN AN INTEGRATED EUROPE

GERMANY has not always been a bad neighbour and in the foreseeable future the countries and peoples which have to live alongside her in Europe may be prepared to accept her as a good neighbour once again. But that is not yet the case. Fear and danger make strange bedfellows, but the fear and danger of Soviet aggression in the years since 1945 have not yet brought the other countries of western and central and northern Europe to the point of letting bygones be bygones and cheerfully permitting Germany to re-arm or even to play a leading role (as her resources of manpower would permit her to do) in the building up of a west European army under the aegis of the North Atlantic Treaty Organization and the European Defence Community. This reluctance on the part of Dutchmen and Frenchmen, Belgians and Danes, Norwegians, Greeks and Yugoslavs, and even of many Italians and Austrians, is resented by some Germans and not very well understood by most of them. Their memories of the years between 1939 and 1945 are perhaps not so sharp as those of their neighbours, for one can forget most easily what one would prefer not to remember.

The attitude of the United States in this matter of Germany's re-armament or participation in a European army tends to add confusion rather than clarity to the situation, and the attitude of Great Britain (when this can be ascertained) is not always very helpful either. These two powers are, in fact, on the horns of a dilemma. Both governments have a reasonable fear and suspicion of Soviet intentions in Europe and the world, but neither is prepared to contemplate keeping large enough armies on the active list to counterbalance the mighty land force that the Soviet Union has maintained in being since 1945. In open warfare atomic power is an almost untried weapon which might easily back-fire in its effects, and as a diplomatic weapon it has so far proved virtually useless to either party. Just as the Second World War was fought without recourse to the use of poison gas or bacteriological warfare by either side, both sides might be equally chary of hurling the first atomic bomb of a third world war. Such a state of uncertainty means that land armies continue to be of great potential importance because there must be somebody physically able to occupy the land even if it has been devastated and rendered radio-active by atomic warfare. A 'push-button war' may be just round the corner, but it *is* still round that corner, and there remains the suspicion that, however many buttons are pushed, the ordinary foot-slogging, crank-turning type of army will still be needed. That is where Germany comes in once again. No country with a population of forty-eight millions (with another eighteen millions in the East German Republic, which might be on one side or might be on the other), situated in the heart of Europe and occupying the potential no-man's-land between east and west, can be ignored or set aside, however much you may dislike those forty-eight (or sixty-six) million people for what they have been doing during the last seventy-five to a hundred years.

Apart from this vexed question of the re-armament

of Germany and German participation in a west European army, there has been some progress in the direction of receiving back Germany into the community of nations since her unconditional surrender and her destruction as a sovereign state in May 1945. The most important steps so far have been her participation as an equal partner in the European Iron and Steel Community under the Schuman Plan, and the re-affirmation in the West German general election of September 1953 of the support for Dr. Conrad Adenauer, whose policy rests upon co-operation with the West to the fullest possible extent, but no abandonment of the campaign for the restoration of full German sovereignty and unity.

How these last two aims are to be achieved lies in the mists of the future. As these words are being written, yet another Four-Power Conference is about to meet to consider, among other things, the future of Germany. For somewhat different reasons all four powers—even the United States—are apprehensive about Germany's future, for they have all suffered acutely from Germany's past. But perhaps the country and the people which have suffered most from Germany's past, and the deficiencies of her leaders at different periods in her history have been Germany and the Germans themselves. Is Germany now at another turning-point in her evolution, at which she will be able to abandon the way of her past aggressions and merge with the European community of peace-loving nations as successfully as have, for instance, the once aggressive Swedes and Swiss, or will she fail to resist the temptation to make herself overly strong once again by playing off the east and the west against each other and thus bestriding the European and world balance of power?

The evolution of Germany up to the present moment

cannot inspire anybody with too much confidence that she will avoid the way of aggression in the future, if given the chance. On the other hand, if the German people *is* able to learn from history that such aggression does not pay, it has surely received enough lessons to that effect over the past forty years.

READING LIST

THIS select list of under a hundred titles is restricted to books that will be found useful for further general study of the subject and are available in English. The books starred contain bibliographies of value in giving guidance for more advanced study. Double-starred books are specially recommended.

1. **General**
    Putzger, F., *Historisches Schul-Atlas.* Contains indispensable maps, but no text (a post-1945 or pre-1934 edition must be used).
    **Dickenson, R. W., *Germany*, 1953. A comprehensive study, basically geographical, but with much historical data. Many excellent maps.
    *Valentin, V., *The German People*, 1946. English translation of a valuable detailed survey.
    Vermeil, E., *Germany's Three Reiches*, 1945. English version of a penetrating French analysis.
    Gooch, G. P., *Studies in German History*, 1948. A collection of characteristically erudite essays.
    Haller, F., *Epochs of German History*. English translation (1930) of a provocatively nationalistic but scholarly German work.
    **Reinhardt, K., *Germany: 2000 Years*, 1950. Roman Catholic viewpoint. Special attention to culture-history. An excellent advanced text-book.
    *Steinberg, S. H., *History of Germany*, 1944. A useful factual survey incorporating results of recent researches, and very careful chronology.

2. **The Reformation and Earlier (to A.D. 1555)**
    **Barraclough, G. (ed.), *Medieval Germany, 911–1250*, 2 vols., 1938. Translations of a number of

important essays by leading German scholars, with a valuable introduction by the editor.

*Barraclough, G., *Origins of Modern Germany*, 1946. A stimulating projection of medieval German history and an attempt to place it in its true perspective. Valuable bibliographical footnotes.

Thompson, J. W., *Feudal Germany*, 1928. A classic.

**The Cambridge Medieval History*, 8 vols., and *The Shorter Cambridge Modern History*, 2 vols. (*passim*).

Chambers's Encyclopaedia, 1950 edition; articles on 'German History' (by A. L. Poole, S. H. Steinberg and J. A. Hawgood) and on 'Prussia: *History*' (by F. L. Carsten); and relevant biographical articles.

**Mosse, G. L., *The Reformation*, 1953. A brief and very helpful essay in the Berkshire Series.

*Brandi, K., *Charles V*, 1939. Translation of the standard biography.

*Wedgwood, C. V., *The Thirty Years War*, 1938. Detailed treatment, but some conclusions challenged by Steinberg (above).

**The Cambridge Economic History*, Vols. I and II (*passim*), are invaluable. No others yet published.

Tacitus, *Germany*, Penguin Classics translation, annotated, 1952. Gives a highly subjective but more or less contemporary Roman view of the primitive Germans.

Brogan, O., *Roman Gaul*, 1953. Helps to restore a balanced view and puts Caesar and Tacitus in their places.

3. **Between the Reformation and the Revolutionary Era (1555–1789)**

Fay, S. B., *Rise of Brandenburg-Prussia to 1786*, 1937. Another concise and useful essay in the Berkshire Series.

*Carsten, F. L., *The Origins of Prussia*, 1954. A scholarly treatment, incorporating latest researches.

Gaxotte, P., *Frederick the Great*, 1941. Translation of a standard continental interpretation.

*Gooch, G. P., *Frederick the Great*, 1947. Matured views of an eminent British authority (to be compared with Gaxotte).

**Bruford, W. H., *Germany in the Eighteenth Century*, 1935. Concentrates on literary movements and trends.

*Willoughby, L. A., *The Classical Age of German Literature, 1748–1805*, 1926. Another valuable literary survey.

Robertson, J. G., *Life of Goethe*, 1927. The standard British biography. Careful and moderate.

*Pascal, R., *The German Sturm und Drang*, 1953. A scholarly analysis of a seminal movement.

Mirabeau, Comte de, *The Prussian Monarchy*, 1788. (A number of English translations exist of this witty, penetrating and biased French attack on Prussia, and on the memory of Frederick the Great, by a master of invective).

4. 1789–1815

*Gooch, G. P., *Germany and the French Revolution*, 1920. Immense erudition wrapped in somewhat bland phraseology. The standard work in English.

*Aris, R., *Political Thought in Germany, 1789–1815*, 1936. Another erudite survey.

**Fisher, H. A. L., *Studies in Napoleonic Statesmanship: Germany*, 1903. An important and stimulating book. Scholarly, yet very good reading.

**Ford, G. S., *Stein and the Era of Reform in Prussia*, 1922. A useful short survey.

*Willoughby, L. A., *The Romantic Movement in Germany*, 1930. A standard literary history.

**Snyder, L. L., *German Nationalism*, 1952. A series of valuable essays on its origin and development.

Also useful for nineteenth- and twentieth-century Germany.

De Stael, Mme, *Germany*, 1813 (English translation 1893). The Tacitus of her day, better informed, but no less splenetic.

Fichte, J. G., *Addresses to the German Nation*, 1807 (English translation 1922, etc.). Another contemporary work of paramount importance. See Snyder (*above*) for a critical analysis of his ideas and influence.

5. **1815–1850**

Taylor, A. J. P., *The Course of German History (since 1815)*, 1945. Written to shock susceptibilities —and succeeds. An anti-traditionalist view.

**Taylor, A. J. P., *The Habsburg Monarchy*. (The 2nd edition, 1948, should be used.)

*Cecil, A., *Metternich*, 1933. A careful appraisal, not over-written, as are most studies of Metternich.

Legge, J. G., *Rhyme and Revolution in Germany, 1813–1850*, 1918. Uneven, but much better than its title would lead one to expect.

*Henderson, W. O., *The Zollverein*, 1939. Standard treatment of an important theme.

Corti, E. (Count), *The Rise* and *The Reign of the House of Rothschild*, 2 vols., 1928. Entertaining account of the great Frankfurt banking family, containing valuable social and economic history.

Goethe, J. W., *Conversations with Eckermann* (English translation in Everyman edition). Superman at grips with the *Zeitgeist*. The Master's mature reflections on his age.

*Brandes, G., *Young Germany*, 1923. A standard treatment.

**Valentin, V., *1848: Chapters in German History*, 1940. Abbreviated translation of his standard two-volume history of the German Revolutions of 1848.

**Namier, L. B., *1848: The Revolution of the Intellectuals*. A mixture of profound erudition and 'debunking' analysis and an essay of major importance.

Carr, E. H., *Karl Marx*, 1938, and *Bakunin*, 1937. Skilful analyses of these two stormy petrels of the Years of Revolution in Germany—and elsewhere.

**Hansen, M. L., *The Atlantic Migration, 1601–1860*, 1940. Specially good for German emigration. Has become the standard work.

*Hawgood, J. A., *The Tragedy of German-America*, 1940. Contains an account of the attempts to found 'New Germanies' in the United States.

*Wittke, C., *Refugees of Revolution*, 1952. The best detailed survey of the German 'Forty-Eighters' in America.

Schurz, C., *Reminiscences*, 1909. His own story, by the most famous of the 'Forty-Eighters'.

6. 1850–1871

Darmstaedter. F., *Bismarck and the Creation of the Third Reich*, 1948. A useful survey.

Friedjung, M., *The Struggle for Supremacy in Germany, 1859–1866*. (Partial translation into English, 1935.)

**Eyck, E., *Bismarck and the German Empire*, 1950. An abbreviated translation of his three-volume 'revisionist' biography published in exile in 1944. (See also his 'Bismarck after Fifty Years' in *Historical Association Pamphlets, General Series, G8*, 1948.)

Robertson, C. Grant, *Bismarck*, 1915. One of the earliest biographies 'this side idolatry', and still useful.

**Clapham, J. H., *Economic Development of France and Germany*, 1923. Contains a valuable account of the nineteenth-century transformation of Germany into a major industrial power.

*Kuczynski, J., *Labour Conditions in Germany from 1880 to the Present Day*, 1945. Specialized study of one important aspect of the great transformation.

Hurst, F. W., *Friedrich List*, 1909. By no means unsympathetic essay on this arch economic nationalist by an eminent British Liberal publicist.

*Kohn-Bramstedt, E., *Aristocracy and Middle Class in Germany*, 1937. A careful sociological analysis.

Newman, E., *Wagner: Man and Artist*, 1924. The standard biography in English of this highly complex and significant figure.

7. 1871-1918

*Brandenburg, E., *From Bismarck to the World War*, 2 vols., 1927. Translation into English of a German 'new-view' (when written) of the era.

Carroll, E. M., *Germany and the Great Powers, 1866–1914*. A useful survey.

Fuller, J. W., *Bismarck's Diplomacy at its Zenith*, 1922. A scholarly analysis.

Redlich, J., *Francis Joseph I*, trans. 1925. Still the best biography available in English.

Davis, H. W. C., *Political Thought of H. von Treitschke*, 1914. An early attempt to interpret and understand ultra-nationalistic German thought and action. To be compared with Snyder (*above*).

Muncy, L. W., *The Junker, 1888–1914*. Analysis of a highly significant group.

*Gooch, G. P., *Recent Revelations of European Diplomacy*, 4th edition, 1940. A distillation of the results of the widespread official publication of diplomatic documents between 1918 and 1939.

Bülow, C. von., *Memoirs*, trans.; 4 vols., 1929–31. William III's least unimportant Chancellor self-revealed.

Bülow, C. von., *Imperial Germany*, trans. 1914.

*Wertheimer, M. S., *The Pan-German League, 1900–1914*, 1924.
**Townsend, M. F., *The Rise and Fall of the German Colonial Empire*, 1930. The standard work.
*Taylor, A. J. P., *Germany's First Bid for Colonies, 1884–1885*, 1931.
*Woodward, W. L., *Great Britain and the German Navy*, 1935.
Naumann, C., *Mittel-Europa*. Trans. as *Central Europe*, 1917. A blue-print of pan-Germanism.
*Schmidt, B., *Coming of the World War*, 1930. An American 'revisionist' spreads the blame somewhat too evenly.
**Rosenberg, Albert, *Birth of the German Republic*. Trans., 1931, of a standard Liberal German account.

10. **Since 1918**

    **Rosenberg, Albert, *History of the German Republic*. Trans., 1936, of a Liberal post-mortem.
    Scheele, G., *The Weimar Republic*, 1946. A shorter and more 'popular' account.
    Wheeler-Bennett, J. W., **Brest Litovsk, the Forgotten Peace, March 1918*, 1938; **Hindenburg, the Wooden Titan*, 1936; and **The Nemesis of Power; the German Army in Politics, 1918–1945*, 1953, are all essential reading for an understanding of the latest epochs in German history. Scholarly, well-written and trenchant.
    Vallentin, A., *Stresemann*. Trans., 1931, of a friendly German biography of this most important figure of the Weimar period.
    Clark, R. T., *Fall of the German Republic*, 1934.
    *Butler, R. D'O., *Roots of National Socialism, 1783–1933*, 1942.
    Hitler, A., *Mein Kampf* (many editions and several translations, 1927ff.), and **Speeches, 1922–1939*,

2 vols., trans. and very fully annotated by N. H. Baynes, 1942. For reference purposes only.

Roberts, S. H., *The House that Hitler Built*, 1937. More scholarly and less popular than it sounds.

The Goebbels Diaries. Trans. by L. Lochner, 1948. Have to be read not to be believed.

Dodd, W. E., *Ambassador Dodd's Diaries, 1933–38*, 1941. A tough, if sometimes naïve, American historian-diplomat in Hitler's Wonderland.

Meinecke, F., *The German Catastrophe*. Trans., 1950, of the post-war second and third thoughts on the events of his age of this veteran German historian.

Wiskeman, E., *The Berlin-Rome Axis*, 1949. Best account yet published of this diplomatic monstrosity.

**Bullock, A., *Hitler: A Study in Tyranny*, 1952. First full-length scholarly biography in English appearing since 1945.

Chambers's Encyclopaedia; World Survey volumes, 1952 and 1954, contain brief accounts of recent developments in Germany.

The Europa Yearbook (loose-leaf, in progress) provides up-to-date statistical and other data upon Germany, continuously under revision.

INDEX

Adenauer, Conrad, 91, 192
Alemanni (Swabians), 23, 44, 57–8, 64, 131, 133
Alsace, 4, 35
Alsace-Lorraine, 91, 95
Arminius ('Hermann'), 69, 127–8
Aufklärung, 159–65, 169
Austria (*see also* Habsburg Dynasty), 18, 19, 25, 30, 85, 92, 95, 106–7, 109, 111, 113, 160, 169, 184
Avars, 25, 135

Baden, 19, 99, 101–2, 107, 113
Baltic Provinces (*and* States), 38–9, 67–8, 179, 180
'Balts' (Baltic Germans), 39, 180
Bavaria, 11, 28, 37, 50, 99, 101–2, 113, 122, 160
Bavarians (*and* Marcomanni), 7, 25, 44, 58, 132
Bismarck, Otto von, 10, 18, 19, 30, 80, 85, 89, 93, 95, 97, 102–5, 106, 108, 110, 119, 153, 174, 175
Black Death, 51, 60, 66, 81
Bohemia (*and* Moravia), 17, 23, 27, 28, 29, 36, 38, 40, 95, 107, 180, 184
Brandenburg (*see also* Prussia), 18, 22–3, 40, 155, 181
Burgundians, 6, 57
Burgundy:
  Duchy, 4, 31, 32, 33, 34, 40
  Kingdom, 31

Carolingian Empire, 7, 9, 11, 47–8, 57–8, 127, 133–8, 139

Charles the Great ('Charlemagne'), 7, 9, 10, 11, 14, 47, 134–8, 139–40
Charles IV (*Emperor*), 73, 141, 155
Charles V (*Emperor*), 141, 150, 171
Charles Eugene (*Duke of Württemberg*), 124–5, 166
Confederation of the Rhine, 113–14, 142
Czechs (*see also* Bohemia), 28–30

Electors (*Imperial*), 65–6
Erasmus, 156, 158

Forster, Georg, 167, 170
France (*and* Germany), 6, 12, 32–4, 58–9, 73, 76, 84, 112–14, 115, 146, 159, 169
Franconia (*and the* Franconians), 7, 11, 34, 58
Franklin, Benjamin, 162, 172
Franks, 5–7, 12, 23, 34, 44, 56, 64, 127, 131
Frederick I ('Barbarossa', *Emperor*), 23, 144–5
Frederick II (*Emperor*), 14, 65, 73, 140, 145–6
Frederick II ('The Great', *King of Prussia*), vi, 76, 118, 120–1, 123, 161–3, 173
Frederick William ('The Great Elector', *of Prussia*), 118, 173
Frederick William I (*King of Prussia*), 118, 161–2

French Revolution (*of 1789*), 76, 166–70
Friesland (*and the* Friesians), 11, 23, 45, 55, 59, 131

Germania (*see also* Tacitus), 127–9
German:
  Class Structure, 55, 57–8, 64–5
  Colonies (*overseas*), 81, 170, 172–8
  Emigration, 82, 84–5, 171–2, 179–89
  Feudalism, 64–5
  Forests, 43–6, 64
  Immigration, 84, 181, 184–5
  Nationalism, 36, 80, 140, 149, 157–8, 162, 164, 167–9, 172, 177, 186–7
  Navy, 176–7
  Population, 46, 57, 78, 81–6, 181, 191
  State (*Idea of*), 13, 14, 91, 93, 95–6, 97, 139–40, 157–8
  [*See also* under *Marks, Towns, Villages, Universities*, etc.]
Germany (*General topics arranged chronologically*):
  Prehistoric, 1–4
  Roman, 5–6, 9–10, 127–32
  Tribal Duchies, 11, 133–5
  Confederation of the Rhine, 113–14, 142
  Confederation (1815), 19, 102, 109–11
  Frankfurt Constitution (1849), 19, 102, 106–8
  North German Confederation (1867), 102
  Weimar Republic (1919), 61, 62, 94, 97–101, 106
  Zones of Occupation (1945), 88 (*map*), 89–90
  East German Republic (1949), 90, 91
  West German Republic (1949), 90–1
  [*See also* under *Saxon, Salian, Hohenstauffen, Luxemburg, Habsburg* and *Hohenzollern Dynasties, Holy Roman Empire, National Socialism*, etc.]
Goethe, J. W. von, 66, 124, 163–5, 166–8
Golden Bull, 14, 66, 141
Gregory VII ('Hildebrand', *Pope*), 143–6

Habsburg Dynasty (*see also* Austria), 18, 33, 40, 83, 107, 114–15, 118, 120–2, 123, 140–2, 174
Hanover (*Electorate and Kingdom*), 18, 19, 105, 125
Hanseatic League, 39, 50, 69–74, 76, 179–80
Hecker, Friedrich, 107, 188
Henry the Fowler (*of Saxony, German King*), 11, 12, 14, 22–3, 24, 32, 91, 137
Henry III (*German Emperor*), 139, 148
Henry IV (*German Emperor*), 13, 140, 144–5
Henry the Lion (*Duke of Saxony*), 65, 71
Herder, J. G. von, 123, 162, 164
Hessen, 107, 113
Hitler, Adolf, 27–8, 30, 62, 80, 89, 93, 96, 100, 143, 163, 177, 184–5
Hohenstauffen Dynasty, 12, 13, 65, 140–1, 145–6
Hohenzollern Dynasty, 40, 94, 97–9, 102–5, 115–19, 174–8, 188

Holy Roman Empire, 33–4, 40, 111, 113, 120, 137, 139–42, 143–8, 150, 156
Hungary (see also Magyars), 27, 29, 36, 122, 180

Industrial Revolution (in Germany), 52, 75–80, 84–5
Innocent III (Pope), 13, 144–5
Italy (and Germany), 32, 48, 50, 69, 135, 141, 155, 173

Joseph II (Emperor), 120, 122–3, 142
Junkers, 61, 62

Kant, Emmanuel, 123, 162, 163, 165

Länder (of Germany):
  1918–33: 90, 93–4
  1933–45: 89, 95
  since 1945: 89–90
Leibnitz, G. W., 161–3
Lessing, G. E., 162–3, 165
Liberation (Era of), 167, 172
Limes (of Roman Empire), 14, 43, 127, 130–1, 133
Lorraine (see also Alsace-Lorraine), 7, 11, 12, 23, 34
Lotharingia (Kingdom of), 31–2, 34, 35, 138 (map)
Louis XIV (and Germany), 83, 119, 183
Luther, Martin, 101, 149–54, 156–7
Luxemburg Dynasty, 141

Magyars, 25, 26
Maria Theresa (Empress), 121–2, 123, 161–2
Marks (or Marches), 23, 25, 26 (map), 179
Maximilian I (Emperor), 33, 140–1, 150, 156
Mecklenburg, 36, 101, 113

Metternich, Prince, 109–10, 120, 125, 170
Mexico (and Germany), 173–4
Mirabeau, Comte de, 122, 165

Napoleon I (and Germany), 30, 77, 109, 112–14, 120, 142, 167, 168, 170
National Socialism, 86, 93–6, 101, 164, 183
Netherlands (and Germany), 31, 35, 73, 115, 122

Otto I ('the Great', Emperor), 25, 139

Palatinate (Electorate), 83, 155, 159, 160, 172
Papacy, 12, 13, 19, 135, 140, 143–8
Pennsylvania (Germans in), 83, 172, 186
Poland (and Germany), 27, 29, 36, 38–9, 40, 68, 91, 95, 122, 180
Pomerania, 23, 36, 38
Preuss, Hugo, 97, 99
Prussia (and the Prussians—see also Brandenburg), 18, 19, 22, 33, 38, 41, 76, 78, 84, 94, 97, 101–2, 103, 109, 111–14, 160, 169–70, 173, 180

Reformation (in Germany), 14, 66, 82, 149–54, 157–8, 160–1
Renaissance (in Germany), 157–8, 159
Rhine-Province (of Prussia), 18, 19
Rosenberg, Alfred, 27, 40, 95
Russia (and Germany):
  Muscovy, 29
  Russian Empire, 29, 30, 39, 115
  Soviet Union, 95, 185, 190–1

Salian Dynasty, 12, 13
Saxe-Weimar-Eisenach (*Duchy of*), 47, 124, 164, 166–8
Saxony, 3, 11, 17, 59, 76, 101, 155, 160
Saxon Dynasty, 12
Saxons, 5, 7, 17, 35, 57, 64, 132, 135
Schiller, F. von, 163, 164–5, 167
Silesia, 3, 23, 36, 38, 77
Stael, Mme de, v, 165
Stalin, Joseph, 30, 185
Stein, Freiherr von, 60, 76, 123
Swabia (*see also* Alemanni), 3, 11, 14
Sweden (*and Germany*), 29, 115, 192
Switzerland (*and Germany*), 31, 35, 73, 104, 107, 192

Tacitus (*see also* Germania), 5, 9, 54–5, 63, 127
Teutonic Knights (*and Order*), 22, 39, 67, 73, 179–80
Thirty Years War, 51, 81–2, 159
Thuringia:
  Tribal Duchy, 3, 11, 12, 17, 34, 44, 57, 59, 64, 132, 133
  Land (1919), 97, 101
Tyrol, 50, 184
Towns (*of Germany*), 36, 39, 43, 47–53, 69–74, 78–9, 82, 85

Aachen, 47, 49
Augsburg, 74, 156
Berlin, 53, 91, 160
Bremen, 101–2, 104
Cologne, 45, 49–50, 52, 53, 67, 71–2, 73
Danzig, 72, 73, 76
Frankfurt-am-Main, 124, 133
Goslar, 48, 49, 70, 71
Hamburg, 72, 76, 101, 102, 104
Heidelberg, 83, 155, 159
Lübeck, 51, 52, 70, 71
Magdeburg, 45, 48, 50, 51
Nürnberg, 70, 74, 156
Vienna, 83, 155, 161
Transylvania (*Germans in*), 38, 180, 186

Universities (*of Germany*), 155–6

Verdun (*Partition of*, 843), 7, 9, 137, 138 (*map*)
Villages (*of Germany*), 56–60
Völkerwanderung, 6–8, 28, 45, 55, 63, 131–4, 179

Wagner, Richard, 43, 56
William II (*German Emperor*), 104, 176–8
Wisconsin (*Germans in*), 84, 186
Württemberg, 99, 101, 102, 112, 124–5, 154, 164, 166

Zollverein, 78.

For Product Safety Concerns and Information please contact our EU
representative GPSR@taylorandfrancis.com
Taylor & Francis Verlag GmbH, Kaufingerstraße 24, 80331 München, Germany

www.ingramcontent.com/pod-product-compliance
Lightning Source LLC
Chambersburg PA
CBHW052110300426
44116CB00010B/1602